Men-at-Arms • 472

Armies of the Irish Rebellion 1798

Stuart Reid • Illustrated by Gerry & Sam Embleton

Series editor Martin Windrow

First published in Great Britain in 2011 by Osprey Publishing,
Midland House, West Way, Botley, Oxford, OX2 0PH, UK
44-02 23rd Street, Suite 219, Long Island City, NY 11101, USA
E-mail: info@ospreypublishing.com

OSPREY PUBLISHING IS PART OF THE OSPREY GROUP

A CIP catalogue record for this book is available from the British Library

Print ISBN: 978 1 84908 507 6
PDF ebook ISBN: 978 1 84908 508 3
ePub ebook ISBN: 978 1 84908 939 5

Editor: Martin Windrow
Page layout by: The Black Spot
Index by Alan Thatcher
Typeset in Helvetica Neue and ITC New Baskerville
Maps by the author
Originated by PDQ Media, Bungay, UK
Printed in China through Worldprint Ltd

11 12 13 14 15 10 9 8 7 6 5 4 3 2 1

Osprey Publishing is supporting the Woodland Trust, the UK's leading
woodland conservation charity, by funding the dedication of trees.

www.ospreypublishing.com

Artist's Note

Readers may care to note that the original paintings from which the
colour plates in this book were prepared are available for private sale.
All reproduction copyright whatsoever is retained by the Publishers.
All enquiries should be addressed to:

www.gerryembleton.com

The Publishers regret that they can enter into no correspondence
upon this matter.

OPPOSITE **An 'Irish Chieftain', by the London satirical artist
and print-maker James Gillray or Gilray (1756?–1815).
It was supposedly drawn from life, but how this could
be true is hard to imagine, and he probably based it upon
contemporary sources. Gillray was familiar with military
costume, since his father was a one-armed veteran of
Fontenoy who was granted a Chelsea Hospital pension.
This appears to be a realistic image of an officer of the
United Irishmen, wearing a wide-brimmed hat with a
feather plume and a field sign of leaves; a short-cut blue
double-breasted jacket with cloth-covered buttons and
wing-style shoulder ornaments; pale brown pantaloons
and soft-topped boots, with a broad civilian belt supporting
a sabre and pistols. (All illustrations in this book are from
the author's collection.)**

ARMIES OF THE IRISH REBELLION 1798

THE UNITED IRISHMEN

On the night of 24 May 1798, the moment that most of Ireland's Protestants had dreaded for a century and a half seemed to have arrived: a secret army was assembling outside Dublin, in readiness to storm the Irish capital at daybreak. In the event, that blow never fell, because a last-minute wave of arrests had already robbed the insurgent army of most of its leaders. Across the rest of Ireland, however, it was a different story. Throughout the long summer that followed, armies marched and countermarched in a haphazard campaign marked by atrocities on both sides – some of them more characteristic of the Thirty Years' War than the Age of Reason.

This book does not attempt to draw up any accounting of these horrors – neither of the shooting of prisoners and hanging of civilians by government troops, nor of the drunken massacres of loyalist prisoners by rebel mobs. It is intended primarily as a guide to the identity, character, uniforms and equipment of the forces involved, which on the government side were mostly seldom-described units of Militia, Yeomanry and Fencibles.

* * *

At that date Ireland was a semi-autonomous possession of the British crown, with a 'lord lieutenant' or royal viceroy presiding uncertainly over a notoriously corrupt and inefficient administration based in Dublin Castle. The Williamite War at the end of the 17th century had placed the entire government of the country in the hands of a relatively tiny Anglo-Protestant elite, and for much of the next hundred years any threat to peace and stability came from rural terrorist groups, sporadically calling themselves 'Whiteboys' or 'Defenders'. In the 1770s, however, the outbreak of the American Revolution saw the radicalization of a hitherto quiescent middle class, and this was soon mirrored among loyalists by the spectacular growth of a Volunteer movement ostensibly created to protect the country from the imminent threat of a French invasion. However, once these loyal Volunteers had been organized, armed and uniformed, they gave the authorities food for thought: where the American colonies had gone, Ireland might well follow, if the discontents caused by longstanding restrictions on trade and the subordination of the Irish Parliament to London were not addressed.

Under the circumstances London had no alternative but to make concessions, at the cost of strengthening the hold of the corrupt oligarchy in Dublin, and of sharpening the frustration of the emergent Catholic middle class, who still remained barred from an active part in public life. Encouraged first by the American example, and then by the French Revolution of 1789, many of the latter – in alliance with politicized Presbyterian colleagues in the North – became involved in a secret revolutionary group calling itself the Society of the United Irishmen.

Formed in 1791, this 'left-wing' organization was pledged to a total overthrow of the existing regime and to the establishment of a French-style republic dedicated to Liberty, Equality and the Rights of Man. 'The 98' is popularly characterized in the conventional terms of a Catholic peasant uprising against the Protestant ascendancy, but it is important to remember that many of its radical leaders – such as

Dublin Castle; the seat of British power in Ireland, and the primary objective of Lord Edward Fitzgerald's abortive coup, was very much an administrative complex rather than a fortress.

Lord Edward Fitzgerald, Wolfe Tone and Bagenal Harvey – were Protestants, who regarded religion as an issue only insofar as they wanted to end the entrenched discrimination against Catholics in public life. However, it was only by making common cause with the landless Catholic peasantry that they were able – on paper at least – to form a large army, which was intended to rise up in concert with a French invasion.

The opportunity seemingly came late in 1796, when a French expeditionary force nearly 15,000 strong sailed into Bantry Bay on the far south-west coast. However, the ship carrying the expedition's leader, Gen Lazare Hoche, was missing; and while the would-be invaders waited for him, first bad weather and then the Royal Navy intervened to prevent a landing. Thoroughly alarmed by this narrow escape, the Irish government effectively imposed martial law from 30 March 1798. Lacking any proper intelligence as to exactly who the potential rebels were and what their plans might be, Dublin set small detachments of English, Welsh and Scots Fencibles, Irish Yeomanry and Militia to root them out all across Ireland. The predominant use of these second-line troops – less disciplined than the Line and, in the case of Irish-raised units, often with their own agendas – contributed to the savagery of these man-hunts and searches.

The counter-insurgency operations – at first in Counties Kildare, Laois, Offaly and Tipperary, and later in Co. Wicklow – were unquestionably brutal and haphazardly targeted, but soon proved to be surprisingly effective. Over April and May 1798 dozens of leaders of the United Irishmen were arrested or forced to flee, and alarming quantities of stockpiled arms were discovered or surrendered. This eventually forced the surviving members of the United Executive to face a stark choice: either to order an uprising without waiting for the return of the French, or else to disband. Tragically, the rebel leaders opted for the former course, committing their followers to a military campaign for which they were neither prepared, organized nor equipped.

CHRONOLOGY OF THE CAMPAIGN

This records only some of the more important events; it would be impractical to include most of the minor skirmishes and local counter-insurgency operations that took place throughout the spring and summer of 1798.

30 March 1798 Viceroy Lord Camden declares country to be in state of rebellion, thus effectively instituting martial law.
25 April General Gerard Lake replaces Sir Ralph Abercrombie as commander-in-chief of Crown forces in Ireland.

Many brutalities were carried out during the 'disarmaments' and hunts for rebel sympathizers during spring 1798. This print shows a Capt Swayne 'pitch-capping' villagers at Prosperous, Co. Kildare – a form of torture in which the victim's head was coated with pitch and then set alight. Unsurprisingly, Swayne himself was an early victim of the uprising. The massacre of the garrison at Prosperous in the early hours of 24 May was one of the rebels' few successes on the first day of the rebellion; about 150 of Swayne's South Cork Militia and troopers from the Ancient British Fencibles were killed, and their quarters were burned down.

The arrest of the 34-year-old Lord Edward Fitzgerald by Maj Sirr and a party of the Dumbarton Fencibles on the night of 19 May; this forestalled an attempted coup in Dublin, and robbed the rebels of any central direction. Fitzgerald had powerful friends both in Dublin and in London; the authorities hesitated before putting a price on his head, but this incentive persuaded a Catholic lawyer to betray him. Fitzgerald ignored an appeal to come quietly, and stabbed two British officers with a dagger – one of them mortally – before Sirr shot him in the shoulder. He died in Newgate Prison, Dublin, on 4 June.

19 May United Irish leader Lord Edward Fitzgerald is wounded while resisting arrest in Dublin. He will die in prison three weeks later.

23–24 May The uprising begins, with assembly of rebel armies in the Midlands and South, and a series of (largely unsuccessful) assaults on military posts around Dublin.

24–25 May Execution of 58 suspected United Irish prisoners in Co. Wexford.

26 May Some 4,000 Midlands rebels are attacked and defeated at Hill of Tara, Co. Meath, by *c.*300 Fencibles and Yeomanry. This defeat prevents the spread of the rebellion northwards from Co. Kildare.

27 May Midlands rebels surrender to Gen Dundas at Knockaulin. About 1,000 Wexford rebels, led by Father John Murphy, defeat 110 North Cork Militia and 20 Yeomanry under Col Foote at Oulart Hill.

28 May Wexford rebels successfully attack Enniscorthy.

29 May Further surrender of Midland rebels at Gibbet Rath, Co. Kildare, ends in massacre of 300-plus prisoners by Dublin Militia, Yeomanry and dragoons led by Gen Duff. British column ambushed and destroyed at Three Rocks, near Wexford.

30 May Wexford town abandoned to rebels, who establish Committee of Public Safety.

31 May Bagenal Harvey appointed commander of insurgent army.

1 June Unsuccessful Wexford rebel attack on Newtonbarry.

4 June British column of *c.*750 men under Col Walpole ambushed and destroyed at Tuberneering by Wexford rebels.

5 June Unsuccessful assault by Wexford rebels on New Ross. Mob massacres 100-plus loyalist prisoners at Scullabogue House. Father Philip Roche replaces Harvey as insurgent commander.

6 June Northern revolt finally breaks out in Antrim and Co. Down.

7 June More than 20,000 Wexford and Wicklow rebels are badly defeated at Arklow, Co. Wicklow, by *c.*1,600 British regulars, Fencibles and Yeomanry under Gen Needham and Col Skerret.

9 June In North, rebel attack on Antrim town led by Henry Joy McCracken ends in crushing defeat. County Down rebels win victory at Saintfield.

12/13 June Some 4,000 Co. Down rebels, led by the Presbyterian Henry Munro, are decisively defeated at Ballynahinch by *c.*2,000 government troops under Gen Nugent, ending the rebellion in the North.

16 June First British regular reinforcements arrive in Dublin Bay.

Impression of the rebel massacre of loyalist prisoners at Scullabogue, Wexford, on 5 June; illustration by George Cruikshank (1792–1878) from William Maxwell's much later *History of the Irish Rebellion 1798* (1845). Note that most of the rebels are depicted in their shirtsleeves; that spring and early summer were unusually warm, and there was no rain for weeks before 19 June.

Contemporary panorama of the battle of Vinegar Hill, outside Enniscorthy, Co. Wexford, on 21 June. Note the rebels massed on the high ground, with small bodies of government troops manoeuvring below. While the rebels were at least as numerous as the c.18,000 troops (led by Gens Lake, Dundas, Needham and Duff) who surrounded their camp, the total included many of their dependents, and only a minority of the men had firearms. Anything between 500 and 1,000 fell during the battle and the subsequent pursuit, but many escaped through a space between the government columns at a place which is still known as 'Needham's Gap'.

19 June Midlands rebels defeated at Ovidstown Hill.

20 June Wexford rebels defeated at Foulk's Mill. Loyalist prisoners massacred on Wexford Bridge by rebels under Thomas Dixon.

21 June Wexford rebels decisively defeated at battle of Vinegar Hill outside Enniscorthy.

6 August General Joseph Humbert finally sails from Rochefort with French expedition to support the rising.

23 August Humbert lands with c.1,100 men at Killala, Co. Mayo.

27 August French/rebel victory at Castlebar over larger force led by Gen Lake, which abandons much equipment.

4 September United Irish leader James Napper Tandy accompanies small French force that sails from Dunkirk.

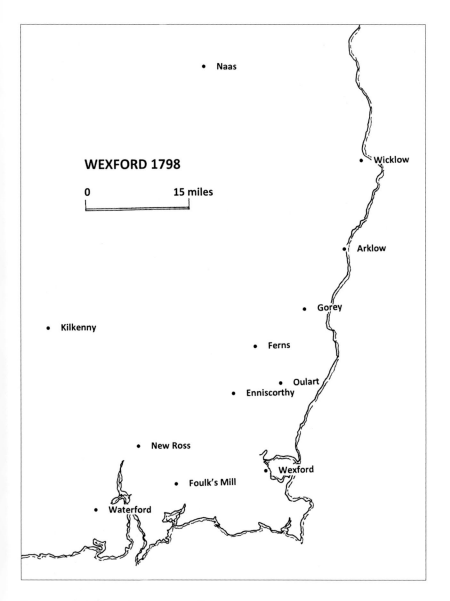

WEXFORD 1798

0   15 miles

- Naas
- Wicklow
- Arklow
- Gorey
- Kilkenny
- Ferns
- Oulart
- Enniscorthy
- New Ross
- Wexford
- Foulk's Mill
- Waterford

5 September French victory at Collooney.

6 September Rebels defeated at Wilson's Hospital near Cavan.

8 September Humbert and main French force intercepted by Gens Cornwallis and Lake, and forced to surrender at Ballinamuck, Co. Longford.

12 September Repulse of fresh rebel assault on Castlebar.

16 September Napper Tandy lands at Rutland Island, Co. Donegal.

17 September Nine French ships with *c.*3,000 troops, and United Irish leader Wolfe Tone, sail from Brest.

23 September Several thousand rebels, with a few French officers, are defeated at Killala by 1,200 government troops under Gen Trench; this effectively marks the end of the campaign.

12 October French ships carrying landing force from Brest are intercepted by Royal Navy fleet under Sir John Warren off Tory Island. Wolfe Tone is captured; he will later cut his own throat after being sentenced to death.

THE BRITISH ARMY

Constitutionally, the British Army belonged to the king but was paid for by Parliament. To be more accurate, however, those regiments serving on the British mainland or overseas were paid for by the mother Parliament in Westminster, and administered by a headquarters situated at the nearby Horse Guards building, while regiments serving in Ireland were instead paid for by the Irish Parliament and directly administered by a local headquarters in Dublin Castle. Other than the Royal Irish Artillery, which was an entirely separate corps from its Woolwich-based counterpart, and four regiments of 'Irish' Horse, units were freely transferred between the British and Irish establishments according to operational or administrative need. While the Irish Establishment was regarded as ultimately subordinate, in that it was subject to rules and regulations promulgated by the Adjutant General in Horse Guards, in actual practice the Irish garrison enjoyed a considerable, and ultimately quite destructive degree of independence.

The peculiarities of the Irish Establishment

The principal reason for this independence was the unique constitutional position of the Irish Establishment. The ordinary existence of the greater part of the Army depended on the passage through Parliament each year of the dramatically-entitled Mutiny Act. This was actually an administrative measure that formally authorized the maintenance of a standing military force over the next 12 months; granted legal authority for the 'articles' or rules and regulations under which it was to operate – hence the 'Mutiny Act'; and, most importantly, specified just how many soldiers would be grudgingly paid for. Except in time of raging war politicians were naturally anxious to reduce military spending, and short of getting rid of the Army entirely (a favourite cry of parliamentarians intent on making a name for themselves), the only way to do that was by cutting it down in size. The first and most obvious way of doing so was through a wholesale disbanding of those regiments considered surplus to immediate requirements on the fortunate outbreak of peace; the other was by reducing the actual numbers of officers and men serving in the regiments that remained.

In Ireland, on the other hand, ever since the reign of King William III and Queen Mary at the end of the 17th century the size of the permanent garrison was fixed by law, first at 12,000 men and then, after 1769, at 15,000, and therefore it did not need to be sanctioned afresh by an annual parliamentary bill. This statutory guarantee meant that throughout the 18th century the Irish garrison served as a convenient refuge for all manner of regiments that might otherwise have been disbanded by the parsimonious Parliament at Westminster.

Unfortunately, the understandable emphasis placed by Dublin Castle on employing the Irish garrison first and foremost to police an unruly population meant that its value as a strategic reserve was compromised, and all too often its units degenerated into little more than a rural gendarmerie of questionable military effectiveness. On the one hand, Ireland was rather better provided than anywhere else with proper barracks in the larger towns, and when posted to them regiments were often able to do some quite useful work. Indeed, the all-important 1792 *Rules and Regulations for the Formation, Field Exercise and Movements of His*

Lieutenant-General Gerard Lake (1744–1808). Appointed to command in Ulster in December 1796, he was promoted commander-in-chief in Ireland on 25 April 1798. Noted for his severity against the rebels, he won the battles of Vinegar Hill and Enniscorthy, but was badly defeated by Gen Humbert at Castlebar.

Majesty's Forces, which were to serve the British Army so well throughout the Napoleonic Wars, were accepted after extensive testing by regiments of the Irish garrison. On the other hand, units could only expect to be rotated into barracks during every second or third year of their service, and they spent far too much of their time scattered far and wide as tiny detachments in villages and country 'police stations'. There they quietly went to seed – to the extent that in the 1750s the Earl of Rothes was moved to issue a stern order that no officer was 'to appear in the Barrack Yard, on the Parade or any where out of doors, in his Night Cap or Slippers'!

It was well known that once posted to Ireland and resigned to the lax control of Dublin Castle, otherwise fine regiments soon went to the dogs. The rot began at the very top, for although the Irish commander-in-chief was appointed by the king, thereafter he answered in the first instance to the king's viceroy in Dublin Castle, and so too did all the officers serving under him. This meant that any attempt to impose real discipline could easily be by-passed by a direct appeal to the viceroy, who was invariably susceptible to political influence in the Castle. Thus, when Gen Abercrombie tried to bring the Army under some proper control with a thoroughly splenetic general order in early 1798, denouncing the scandalous breakdown in discipline which made it 'formidable to all but the enemy' (by which he meant the French), the viceroy was promptly leant upon; Abercrombie was forced to resign, and thereafter it was business as usual.

THE LINE REGIMENTS

Aside from these disciplinary problems, there was the more straightforward one of manpower. On the outbreak of war with France in February 1793 the British Army had only some 50,000 men, largely employed in overseas garrisons. Apart from the cavalry, artillery and Footguards, its disposable strength at the outset theoretically amounted to just 77 regiments of infantry; of these the 1st (Royal) Regiment boasted two battalions, the 60th (Royal Americans) four, and the rest one battalion apiece, making a grand total of 81 battalions of the Line. Moreover, in February 1793 less than one-third of these were immediately available for operational service in continental Europe. No fewer than 19 battalions were serving out in the West Indies; 25 more were scattered between other fixed garrisons in Ireland, Gibraltar, Nova Scotia and the Canadas; and a further nine were serving half a world away in India.

Just 28 infantry battalions were stationed in mainland Great Britain and the Channel Islands, and hardly any of them could be released for operations at short notice. Some of these battalions were still in the ordinary course of rebuilding and retraining after lengthy tours of duty overseas, and were therefore quite unfit for service. Most of the others were unavoidably required for the ordinary defence of the realm, as garrisons and for the guarding of dockyards and other key points, and for maintaining public order as and when necessary. In time some of these duties would be assumed by the yet-to-be-embodied Militia, but for the moment there were just a bare handful of units available. A sudden French thrust towards Antwerp had to be countered by the dispatch of three battalions of Footguards, not because they were the best (in fact, most were shockingly drunk when they embarked), but because they were the only troops immediately to hand.

A field officer of the 1st (Royal) Regiment, after William Loftie. Note the gold-embroidered buttonholes – a privilege enjoyed by those of the regiment's officers who cared to afford it.

A battalion company officer of the 1st (Royal) Regiment, in a print by Dayes, 1792. Like the Loftie drawing, this classic image of the late 18th-century British infantry officer was partly obsolete by 1798, although the elegantly cut-away coat was still seen in many illustrations, particularly of Volunteer and Militia units.

The 1790s manpower shortage

The 15,000 men serving in Ireland – nearly one-third of the Army's total strength in February 1793 – therefore represented a vitally important resource, and orders immediately began to be issued for their recall to the mainland. However, their manning levels presented further problems. Although the old practice of maintaining the Irish battalions at significantly lower strength than those on the British Establishment (in order to cram in as many units as possible, and avoid disbandments) had ended in 1770, from 1788 the official peacetime strength of all infantry battalions stood at just 370 rank and file mustered in ten companies, including one of grenadiers and one of light infantry. The Irish battalions were successfully averaging about 90 per cent of this authorized strength at the beginning of the 1790s (slightly better than those on the British Establishment); but the outbreak of war with France in February 1793 immediately saw this modest establishment more than doubled, quite literally at the stroke of a pen, to 850 men per battalion. The inevitable result of this necessary increase was that in order to bring the service battalions up to their full war strength at short notice it was necessary to strip the additional 500 men from other units not yet given their marching orders. This meant that they in turn were reduced to bare cadres largely composed of the halt, the lame and the untrained, and were thus left in a parlous state of inefficiency.

The problem of bringing these skeleton battalions back up to anything like their required strength, let alone ensuring that they were once again fit for service, was compounded by the fact that for security reasons the regiments carried on the Irish Establishment had always been forbidden to recruit in that country, and instead had to find their men in England or Scotland. Notoriously, some recruiting officers had evaded this prohibition by clandestinely shipping Irish would-be enlistees over to Scotland before attesting them and bringing them back across the North Channel by the next boat; but that had been in peacetime. Now, in the midst of the greatest and most chaotic recruiting boom Britain would see before the creation of Kitchener's New Armies in 1914, the units in Ireland faced crippling competition on both sides of the water – not only from other regiments as desperate as themselves, but also from a whole host of officers and would-be officers 'recruiting for rank' in new companies and battalions. The Catholic Relief Act of 1793 lifted the old ban on enlisting non-Protestants, and was the means of finding tens of thousands of willing recruits in Ireland over the next 20 years and more; but nearly all of them went into units based on the mainland, or straight into newly authorized corps (such as the Irish Brigade – see Plate A2). No sooner were these latter completed than they were transferred out of Ireland and onto the British Establishment.

In theory, of course, the Irish-recruited units could be replaced in turn by other regiments newly raised in Scotland or England, or by those rotated home for rebuilding after service overseas. But the very fact that the newly raised units were complete or very nearly so meant that instead of settling down – as they ought to have done – to a lengthy period of garrison duty and training, they were usually the first to be shipped straight out again irrespective of their actual state of efficiency. The 79th (Cameron) Highlanders were typical; accepted as complete at Stirling on 3 January 1794, they were immediately posted to Belfast, only to be ordered out to Flanders that August. Their state of readiness may be gauged by the fact that they landed at Vlissingen with only one officer to each company, and just eight rounds of ball ammunition for each man.

Conversely, like the original garrison regiments, those veteran units posted back to Ireland after service overseas were invariably in a deplorable condition, and took literally years to recover. Here the experience of the 6th (1st Warwickshire) Regiment of Foot is typical. After a destructive tour in the pestilential West Indies, the regiment was ordered to turn over its effectives to units remaining in theatre, while the officers and NCOs returned home in 1795 to rebuild it. Due to the ordinary difficulty of finding any new recruits in the first place, and then of replacing those that were constantly being drafted away into other units, the regiment was still not properly fit for service when the Irish rebellion broke out three years later. Indeed, the detachment that fought against the French at Castlebar in August 1798 (see Plate E2) was tellingly referred to as a 'remnant'.

The stark fact of the matter was that the regulars who ought to have formed the bedrock of the Crown forces in Ireland were invariably badly under-strength and under-trained. Recognizing this reality, the government's answer was to levy a County Militia.

Drummer and fifer of Footguards wearing 1798-pattern jackets, as depicted by William Pyne; two battalions of Footguards were shipped across to Waterford as part of the reinforcements that landed in June. Note the fifer's elaborately dressed hair, curved sword and brass fife-case.

THE MILITIA

The Militia was initially conceived by the Dublin Castle administration as a purely Protestant force, whose primary duty would be to maintain the existing order and prevent unrest. However, London decreed otherwise; under the Irish Militia Act of 1793, passed just days after the Catholic Relief Act, all men from 18 to 45 years of age, regardless of religion, became liable to serve a four-year enlistment period within Ireland (albeit outside their home counties). The necessary orders were issued by the viceroy towards the end of April 1793, and quotas were assigned to each county and county borough. These had to draw up lists of all those eligible to serve, and then, if necessary, hold ballots to raise their contributions to the required national total of 15,000 men. Voluntary enlistment was permitted from the outset, and so too was the hiring of substitutes, while conversely a fine of £10 was levied on anyone who was drawn by ballot but refused to serve – and in the event of his being unable or unwilling to pay up, he would find himself charged with mutiny.

A crude contemporary caricature of United Irishmen in training, by Gillray; unlike that on page 3, this savage depiction shows them as ape-like figures.
It is of most interest in that it shows, left, a Militia or Yeomanry uniform with a Tarleton helmet being used for target practice.

Not unexpectedly, these measures produced mixed but generally hostile reactions. The landed gentry who were to command the Militia saw it as a source of prestige and patronage, and there was little difficulty in finding the required numbers of officers from among aristocrats, 'opulent farmers' and their sons. However, those who would form the rank and file often took a very different view. In Dublin itself the city Militia regiment was almost entirely recruited by voluntary enlistment; but in the countryside rioting was a more common reaction, and over a period of eight weeks no fewer than 230 people were reported killed during violent protests against the ballots (rather more than in the whole previous century of sporadic disorder). Nevertheless, the regiments were duly formed, and by the close of 1793 some 9,600 men out of the projected 15,000 had been enlisted – but for any future augmentation the balloting process was quietly abandoned.

Willing or otherwise, the rank and file serving in these regiments were described as being 'composed of stout men in the prime of life, drawn almost entirely from the Irish peasantry, inured to labour in the fields, to every vicissitude of climate'. As the great numbers of their compatriots who were even then being enlisted into the regular army ably demonstrated, such men could make excellent soldiers – providing that they were given proper training and leadership. Unfortunately, the operational requirement to scatter the Militia around the countryside in small detachments on police duties for most of the time meant that their training was effectively confined to platoon or at best company level, which may have afforded them a certain facility in weapon-handling but very little else. Their officers were effectively as ignorant as themselves, being commissioned directly into their posts as company and battalion commanders without the necessity of passing through the subaltern ranks to get there. Charles Vallancey, the commander of the Tyrone Militia, grumbled that his officers had no sense of duty, and were only interested in 'walking the streets of Strabane and lounging in the mess room'; while Robert ('Black Bob') Craufurd fumed in his usual forthright manner that 'everyone knows what a brute the uneducated son of an Irish farmer or middleman is'.

This combination of often reluctant conscripts and a negligent officer corps would have been bad enough; but the inevitable fact that the first were largely Catholics and the latter overwhelmingly Protestants gave the leaders of the United Irishmen some cause to hope that a substantial part of the Militia might go over to them. The Limerick, Queens County and Westmeath Militia in particular were confidently considered to be ripe for defection when the signal was given to rise, and the rebels' planned seizure of Dublin was partly predicated on the hope that the Militia would rally to the cause as soon as they were deployed against the insurgents.

These hopes would be disappointed. Surprisingly enough, given its sometimes unpromising composition, the Militia not only overwhelmingly remained loyal, but often proved to be more ruthless than the Yeomanry – as the Dublins demonstrated at Gibbet Rath. Inevitably there were individual exceptions, but, having spent months before the uprising engaged on one side of a vicious counter-insurgency campaign, most militiamen had no inclination to suddenly change sides, no matter that the rebels were often their co-religionists. If they sometimes performed badly in battle there was nothing unique in that, and despite their lack of proper training they did generally stand and fight, even against the French. While the Kilkenny Militia were amongst the first to bolt at Castlebar, Gen Humbert made a point of praising the behaviour of the Longfords, and Charles Vereker's stand with the Limerick City Militia against overwhelming odds at Collooney earned him a viscountcy.

Officer of Light Dragoons or Yeomanry cavalry, after Bunbury. He wears a long hussar-style jacket or 'kitt' – not a regulation garment, but apparently a popular one.

Regiments and facing colours

As was customary when a number of units were authorized on the same date, regimental seniorities were decided by ballot. Initially there were 38 single-battalion regiments, as set out below, all following the same ten-company organization as regular units. Initially the pattern of their uniforms and equipment also adhered closely to that of the regular army: large cocked hats; red tail-coats variously faced in yellow, white, blue, black, or occasionally green (though for some reason, not buff); and white waistcoats and breeches. As discussed in the commentary to Plate B, the Militia seem to have been slow in conforming to subsequent changes in style.

Regiment	Facings	Notes
1. Monaghan	white	see Plate B2
2. Royal Tyrone	blue	Fusiliers 1798
3. North Mayo	yellow	
4. Kildare	black	
5. Louth	green	
6. Westmeath	yellow	Volunteers 1798
7. Antrim	yellow	see Plate B1
8. Armagh	white	
9. North Down	blue	
10. Leitrim	yellow	
11. Galway	yellow	
12. Dublin City	blue	
13. Limerick City	yellow	
14. Kerry	yellow	
15. Longford	blue	Prince of Wales' Longford Militia
16. Londonderry	yellow	see Plate B3
17. Royal Meath	blue	
18. Cavan	black	
19. King's County	blue	
20. Kilkenny	yellow	
21. Limerick County	blue	
22. Sligo	green	
23. Carlow	yellow	
24. Drogheda	green	amalgamated with Louth 1797
24. South Down	blue	
25. Queen's County	blue	
26. Clare	yellow	
27. Cork City	blue	
28. Tipperary	yellow	
29. Fermanagh	yellow	
30. South Mayo	white	
31. Roscommon	black	
32. South Cork	white	
33. Waterford	yellow	Volunteers 1798
34. North Cork	yellow	
35. Dublin County	white	
36. Donegal	black	
37. Wicklow	yellow	
38. Wexford	yellow	Volunteers 1798

THE YEOMANRY

In Scotland and England the embodied forces of the Crown – regulars, Fencibles and Militia – were supplemented by an enthusiastic Volunteer movement, comprising locally-based units of patriotic part-timers authorized and administered by the Home Office rather than by Horse Guards.

Ireland was different. With unhappy memories of the earlier Volunteer movement, the government quickly proscribed those few associations still in existence at the outset of war with France in 1793 (a sensible move, given that they were seemingly dominated by men who had taken the United Irish oath), and until August 1796 refused to sanction the raising of any new ones. The outward justification for the change of heart at that point was the pessimistic perception that in the event of a French invasion so many of the Militia would be occupied in ordinary policing duties that only some 7,000 men out of a theoretical total of 40,000 in the Irish garrison would actually be available for military operations. It therefore followed that if local corps could be formed to assume some of those policing duties, as in Scotland and

England, the greater part of the Militia would be available for deployment against any French landing force.

In mainland Britain a distinction was made by terming mounted units as Yeomanry if raised in the countryside (these being theoretically composed of yeoman farmers and their sons), and as Light Horse Volunteers if formed in towns, while all infantry units were termed Volunteers irrespective of their origin. In Ireland, however, due to its unfortunate political connotations, the latter term was carefully avoided, and all units were designated as Yeomanry irrespective of origin or whether or not they were mounted.

As a secondary aim, the formation of officially sanctioned Yeomanry units was perhaps also seen as a means of exercising a measure of control over some of the wilder elements who were spontaneously beginning to form sectarian militias. A famous example was the Inch Yeomanry, which was entirely composed of members of Lodge 430 of the Orange Order. However, notwithstanding the popular view of the Yeomanry, this was exceptional rather than typical – even in the North, where the nascent Order was strongest – and the evidence actually suggests a much more complex picture. In Omagh, for example, one observer reported an attendance of nearly 2,000 people in a Presbyterian meeting house, and commented: 'The greatest spirit of loyalty and of resistance to the French and Belfast principles were aroused and appeared among them'. Conversely, however, the radicalized Protestants of Belfast, where those dangerous principles were most in evidence, showed much less enthusiasm: Col Lucius Barber wrote in January 1797 that a Yeomanry corps had been got together there consisting of about 150 men, 'such as they are', and grumbled that 'much intrigue and interest was employed to collect even that number'. In some districts an effort was even made to encourage Catholics to join up. At a public meeting to discuss the formation of a Yeomanry corps at Lismore, Co. Waterford, in October 1796, Sir Richard Musgrave noted that 'most of the persons present were papists; which shows how much popularity Grattan and his good coadjutors [leaders of the United Irishmen] have acquired among the honest, the sober and industrious papists of Ireland'. Encouraging Catholic involvement in the Yeomanry was undoubtedly sensible, but it did lead to fears of infiltration by radical elements.

As in the case of the Militia, some of the insurgent leaders hoped that their shortage of military expertise and arms might be alleviated by attracting men from the Yeomanry, and while largely disappointed by the Militia these hopes were sometimes fulfilled by the Yeomanry. Religious issues aside, as part-timers living at home they were very susceptible to local influences, and many of them, having being encouraged to join up to fight the French, were dismayed to find themselves being employed to harass their neighbours. A surprising number consequently took the United oath, whether from political conviction, religious sympathy or other motives, and actually pledged themselves to join the rebels when the time came. For example, the attack on Prosperous on the first night of the rebellion was led by Dr John Esmonde, the second-in-command of the Sallins Yeomanry; while two of the rebel commanders at Oulart, Edward Roche and Morgan Byrne, were still wearing their red Yeomanry jackets on the day of the battle.

Trooper of the 7th Light Dragoons, as illustrated in Le Marchant's 1796 manual on the sword exercise for cavalry. He still wears the relatively loose jacket rather than the hussar-style dolman prescribed in that year.

This Light Dragoon, from Warnery's book on cavalry tactics, provides a good view of the tight jacket with horizontal braiding that was in process of replacing the much looser styles depicted in Le Marchant's book.

The rank and file were equally susceptible to defection, and many of the prisoners executed out of hand in the panic that followed the outbreak of the rebellion were in fact members of the Yeomanry who had earlier been arrested for real or suspected United connections. Startlingly, nearly all of the Seaforde Yeomanry were alleged at one point to have taken the United Irish oath, seemingly on the strength of the fact that their commander, Col Forde, was a well-known liberal and critic of the government. This malicious report prompted hysterical demands to disband the corps and redistribute its arms to more reliable units; but when the then Ulster commander, Gen Lake, investigated the matter for himself, he cheerfully advised the Castle that it was all nonsense and that only two men had in fact taken the oath. Forde continued to be regarded with a rather jaundiced eye by the political establishment, but nevertheless retained his command, and at Ballynahinch his corps served creditably enough to earn Gen Nugent's warm commendation.

While the larger Yeomanry units originally boasted both infantry and cavalry, most were little more than independent troops or companies of either, and, although once numerous, by and large the infantry element fell away in the years after the rebellion. Not surprisingly, proper training was virtually non-existent, and some units only received their arms and accoutrements on the very eve of the uprising. Consequently the Yeomanry were generally poorly disciplined, and their reputation was not improved by the formation during the rising of what were termed Supplementary Yeomanry units; these were raised for the duration of the emergency, and were enthusiastically guilty of what would now be regarded as 'ethnic cleansing' and war crimes. On the other hand, however, the fact that the uniformed Yeomanry were quite literally defending their own homes meant that they often fought bravely, and provided vital local knowledge of both the countryside and the people.

Uniforms and equipment
The little information available suggests that while the Supplementary Yeomanry simply wore their own everyday riding clothes and carried whatever arms they pleased or could borrow, the established Yeomanry units were dressed very similarly to their Volunteer counterparts on the mainland. Both cavalry and infantry units wore red jackets or coats, usually faced with red, blue or yellow. The Loyal Dublin Cavalry, for example, decided in 1797 that their full dress was to be a scarlet coat with blue collar and cuffs and white turnbacks, with four pairs of silver twist loops on both coat and waistcoat, and red shoulder wings decorated with silver chain. As a matter of course cavalry units wore Tarleton helmets, decorated in the case of more well-to-do units with 'leopardskin' turbans. The Yeomanry infantry corps probably followed their mainland counterparts in wearing the same, or fur-crested 'round' hats, rather than the unpopular military cocked hat. Infantry units had firelocks and bayonets, and cavalry units

were issued with swords, but apparently carbines were not regarded by Dublin Castle as a priority. In terms of equipment, both sorts of unit appear to have received the necessary accoutrements to accompany their weapons, but not items such as knapsacks, blankets, and 'camp equipage' – haversacks and canteens.

THE FENCIBLES

Given the all-too-obvious deficiencies of the conscript Militia and volunteer Yeomanry, and the alarming shortage of regulars, Dublin Castle's principal reliance had to be placed on Scottish and English Fencible regiments.

The Fencibles had their origin in Scotland, where the absence of a statutory militia required the hasty creation of home-service regiments on the outbreak of war. These forerunners of the later Territorial Army could only be employed for the defence of the realm, and could not be sent overseas without their consent. As such they were at first really Militia regiments in all but name, differing from their English counterparts only in so far as they were entirely raised by voluntary enlistment rather than conscription. Thus the original six battalions were only required to serve within Scotland except in case of an actual French invasion (and an attempt to send them to England foundered amidst a flurry of protest, culminating in a noisy but bloodless mutiny). Consequently, when more regiments were authorized it was stipulated that their service could be extended beyond Scotland to anywhere within the British Isles. This meant that, unlike English Militia regiments, they could be posted to Ireland. While realization of this happy fact provided sufficient impetus for the raising of similar English, Welsh and even Irish Fencible regiments, it was the 'Scotch Fencibles' who were seen to dominate the Irish garrison in the latter part of the 1790s.

Outwardly they were virtually indistinguishable from regulars, being organized, clothed, equipped and trained in exactly the same manner; however, officers' commissions could not be purchased, and their half-pay (and pensions for the rank and file) was only granted if injured on active service. The Fencibles also differed significantly from the Militia in that it was insisted that they should have at least a leavening of regular officers taken from the half-pay list; for example, James Urquhart transferred from the half-pay of the 14th Foot to command the Essex Fencibles. Moreover, the adjutants of Fencible units – such as Aaron Blanche, who led the Reay Fencibles at the Hill of Tara – were usually, if not invariably, commissioned ex-regular NCOs.

Regiments and uniforms

The following Fencible battalions served in Ireland during the rebellion. In a number of cases uniform details are unknown, but there sometimes appears to be a correlation between the facing colours displayed by

Detail from Thomas Robinson's contemporary painting of the battle of Ballynahinch, now in the National Gallery of Ireland. This shows the captured insurgent 'Colonel' McCulloch about to be summarily executed by Irish Yeomanry. The three Yeomen in the foreground wear dark blue jackets faced red at collar, shoulder straps and cuffs, with white trim and silver buttons, and Tarleton helmets. The standing and mounted figures in the middleground and background have red jackets faced dark blue. The troopers are shown armed only with sabres, not with carbines. The doomed rebel officer's costume is partly reconstructed as Plate G3: a tailcoat, pantaloons and waistcoat of three differing shades of light brown, the coat with a red stand-and-fall collar. He also wears a green neckcloth, and deeply turned-down 'jockey' boots.

Another detail from Robinson's Ballynahinch painting, showing Militia and Yeomanry officers and men grouped around the dying Capt Evatt. The officer at far left, in dark blue pantaloons and half-gaiters, seems to wear a short-tailed jacket of the October 1797 pattern, and the officer next to him in white pantaloons and knee-length gaiters has the light-infantry style without the rear turnback, which would become the new 1799 pattern. Robinson shows other figures wearing the older style of long-tailed coat.

regular, Fencible and Militia units drawn from or at least associated with particular areas.

Most of the Scottish battalions are recorded as wearing Highland dress in one form or another, but this was an uncertain quantity (see commentary to Plate D, below). Those marked in the alphabetical list with an asterisk* are definitely known to have had kilts. However, this was reckoned the prime cause of a high sickness rate in the Elgin Fencibles amongst others, and consequently kilts were often reserved for formal occasions, with tartan trews or even plain trousers being the more common order of dress for ordinary duties and on active service.

Infantry battalions
Princess of Wales' Aberdeen Fencibles – yellow facings, Highland dress
Angus Fencibles – yellow facings, bonnet and trews
Duke of York's Banffshire Fencibles – facings probably yellow, Highland dress
Caithness Legion – yellow facings, bonnet and trews
Devon and Cornwall Regiment of Fencible Infantry

Dumbarton Fencibles – black facings, bonnet and trews or kilt*
Loyal Durham Regiment of Fencible Infantry – green facings
Lord Elgin's Fencibles – green facings, Highland dress*
Loyal Essex Regiment of Fencible Infantry – buff facings (see Plate D3)
Fife Fencibles – yellow facings, not in Highland dress
Fraser Fencibles – black facings, Highland dress (see Plate D2)*
Glengarry Fencibles – yellow facings, Highland dress; to Ireland 1798
Inverness-shire Highlanders – buff facings, Highland dress; became
   Duke of York's, and granted blue facings, 1798
Royal Lancashire Volunteers (Fencibles) – blue facings?
Leicester or The Prince of Wales His Regiment of Fencible Infantry
2nd Royal Manx Fencibles – blue facings, fur-crested round hats
North Lowland Fencibles – green facings, may have worn trews
Northampton Regiment of Fencible Infantry – blue facings, red collar
Northumberland Regiment of Fencible Infantry
Loyal Nottingham Regiment of Fencible Infantry – green facings
Reay Fencibles – light blue facings, Highland dress
   (see Plate D1)*
Loyal Somerset Regiment of Fencible Infantry –
   yellow facings
Suffolk Regiment of Fencible Infantry
York Regiment of Fencible Infantry

In addition to the infantry, there were also a number of small Fencible cavalry units serving in Ireland during the rebellion, including two Irish units raised in 1794 – the 1st Fencible Cavalry, otherwise known as Lord Roden's Dragoons, and Lord Glentworth's 2nd Fencible Cavalry. Generally speaking the British-raised Fencible cavalry units were much smaller than their regular counterparts, but, given their primary role as gendarmerie, this was not necessarily a handicap.

Cavalry units
Ancient British Fencible Cavalry (6 troops)
Dumfries Fencible Cavalry (4 troops)
Loyal Essex Fencible Cavalry (6 troops)
Midlothian Fencible Cavalry (2 troops)
Romney Fencible Cavalry (1 troop)
Duke of York's Fencible Cavalry (2 troops)

The two Irish units were seemingly dressed from the outset in dark blue jackets with the usual white cords and lace, fur-crested Tarleton helmets, and white breeches. Roden's 'Foxhunters' had white facings according to Hamilton-Smith's list (although two surviving cornets are coloured light buff), while the 2nd Fencibles had yellow, displayed on collar, cuffs and the helmet turban. The mainland units, by contrast, were originally ordered in April 1794 to be dressed in red jackets; but in

Highland piper, by Pyne. Most letters of service for Highland units substituted two pipers for the fifers traditionally assigned to the grenadier company, and most battalion companies had them too – at the expense of the officers, and often dressed in officers'-quality uniforms, as seen here. The majority of the Scottish Fencible regiments employed in Ireland wore Highland dress in some form or other. (One of Cruikshank's illustrations also shows an Irish bagpiper among a group of rebels.)

'The Fraser sentinel at Castlebar' – detail from Cruikshank's portrayal of a famous incident, when the sentry guarding the jail remained at his post amidst the rout of Lake's army. This provides an intriguing depiction of the uniform of the Fraser Fencibles; kilts were seemingly reserved for full dress, but plain linen trousers were normally worn instead of the tartan trews shown here (see Plate D2).

1798 the Adjutant General's department instructed that they were to wear blue when in Ireland, presumably in order to distinguish them from the red-jacketed Yeomanry. Consequently, the Ancient British Fencibles (from Wales) were described as 'dressed in blue, with much silver lace'.

Other government units

Once the rebellion got underway, particularly in Co. Wexford, it quickly became apparent that the garrison was going to be inadequate for the task of suppressing it, let alone dealing with the anticipated French landing. Reinforcements were urgently required, and consequently a rather mixed collection of units found themselves being shipped across. On 16 June 1798 the 100th Foot (shortly to become the 92nd Highlanders) were the first to land in Dublin. Those sent to Waterford included two battalions of Footguards under Lord Dalhousie; a mercenary cavalry regiment, Hompesch's Mounted Rifles; and a motley band of other foreign mercenaries who were in the process of becoming the 5/60th Regiment. While the latter undoubtedly lent an exotic air to the proceedings (and gained a particularly unsavoury reputation), the principal differences between the reinforcements and those units already serving in the garrison were that they were properly trained, and actually served together as formed battalions rather than being scattered as detachments.

THE REBELS

The enduring image of the rebel armies of 1798 is of dun-coloured masses of pikemen, and the classic description of them was penned by a Wexford loyalist named Charles Jackson:

> *We passed through crowds of rebels, who were in the most disorderly state, without the least appearance of discipline. They had no kind of uniform but were most of them in the dress of labourers, white bands round their hats and green cockades being the only marks by which they were distinguished. They made a most fantastic appearance, many having decorated themselves with parts of the apparel of ladies, found in houses they had plundered. Some wore ladies' hats and feathers, others, caps, bonnets and tippets. From the military they had routed they had collected some clothing which added to the motley show. Their arms consisted chiefly of pikes of an enormous length, the handles of many being sixteen or eighteen feet long. Some carried rusty muskets. They were accompanied by a number of women shouting and huzzaing for the Croppies and crying, 'Who now dare say "Croppies, lie down?"'* [1]

---

1 'Croppies' was a common slang term for the rebels. It may have originated in their radical leaders' penchant for cutting their hair short *à la Titus* in true revolutionary style, or simply in the country practice of wearing the hair short rather than long.

According to some eyewitnesses, when rebel forces were on the march it was if the whole countryside was on the move, and to an extent, particularly in Wexford, this really was the case. The rebels were drawn from almost every level of society and, as noted by Jackson, they were frequently accompanied by wives, sweethearts and dependents. The bulk of them were landless labourers and, except in the North, they were overwhelmingly Catholic; but they also included small farmers and tradesmen, some of whom were United men by conviction, and others men who were driven to join the rebellion by the excesses of the government forces.

Their commanders, and a few individuals besides, found themselves horses to ride, but there were no rebel cavalry units of any description, and no effective artillery. Those few cannon they possessed or captured may occasionally have made an encouraging noise, but otherwise were ineffective, and to all intents and purposes the rebel armies were entirely comprised of infantry.

Weapons

Despite the encouragement offered by France, practical assistance was virtually non-existent, and there is no evidence of any attempt to run guns to the rebels other than during Hoche's abortive expedition in 1796 and Humbert's slightly more successful attempt in August 1798. Consequently, the rebels were entirely thrown back upon their own resources. There were some firelocks and even a couple of cannon hidden away from Volunteer days; a rash of robberies aimed at stealing arms from gentlemen's houses had been carried out in the early months of 1798, and once the rebellion broke out some 'stands of arms' were captured from government troops; but this was sufficient to arm only a bare handful of the thousands sworn to the movement. Entirely typically, after the fight at Naas on the first night of the uprising 800 pikes were picked up from the field but hardly more than 20 firelocks

Impression of rebels plundering a large country house, by Cruikshank; although they date from a generation after the rebellion, much of the detail in his illustrations appears to be authentic. His groups of insurgents often include one or two men wearing uniforms and accoutrements that identify them as defected members of the Yeomanry or Militia.
What appears to be a shako worn by the soldier pounding the keyboard (lower right) might be an anachronism, but on the other hand a variety of odd-shaped caps were worn by light infantry and sometimes grenadiers at this time.

Cruikshank's depiction of an unsuccessful rebel attack on an outpost at Clonard is remarkable for the number of firearms and the accoutrements to go with them.

(though one must remember that men running away from a battlefield are a good deal more likely to throw away pikes than muskets).

The only practical way to procure anything like sufficient weapons for the regiments being secretly raised all across the countryside was by setting local blacksmiths to forging pike-heads – and according to a rebel leader named Miles Byrne, 'almost every blacksmith was a United Irishman'. In some areas the arms seizures by the security forces compelled many rebels to fall back on pitchforks, scythes and other improvisations when the rebellion actually began, but otherwise pikes predominated. According to contemporary descriptions they varied from 10ft to as much as 18ft in length, with handles generally cut from ash, and the heads occasionally embellished with a hook intended to cut harness or pull riders from their horses.

In tactical terms, the widespread use of polearms rather than muskets was not necessarily a crippling disadvantage. Even if the rebels could have provided themselves with sufficient firearms they would still have lacked the training and practice to trade volleys successfully with the Fencibles or even perhaps the Militia. Giving them pikes compelled them to employ offensive tactics akin to the volley-and-bayonet-charge doctrine developed by the regulars during the American War, or the Highland charge of half a century earlier. Certainly, in those instances – as at Enniscorthy – when the rebels succeeded in launching heavy columns of pikemen covered by skirmishers against government forces obligingly drawn up in the open, then raw courage and sheer weight of numbers

(continued on page 33)

It was not only the manorhouses of the rich that attracted rebels bent on plunder; this contemporary caricature by Gillray showing the looting of a farmhouse is probably accurate enough in its essentials. Eyewitnesses – including some who were sympathetic to the United Irish cause – lamented the wanton violence and pointless destruction that always followed when rebels got hold of alcohol. There were honourable instances of priests and educated leaders trying to save victims from the mobs, but often failing.

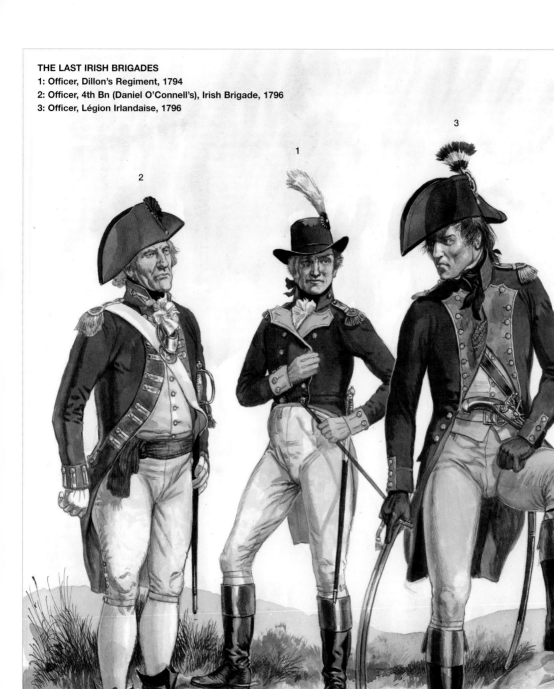

THE LAST IRISH BRIGADES
1: Officer, Dillon's Regiment, 1794
2: Officer, 4th Bn (Daniel O'Connell's), Irish Brigade, 1796
3: Officer, Légion Irlandaise, 1796

IRISH MILITIA, 1798
1: Sergeant-Major, Antrim Militia
2: Private, flank company, Monaghan Militia
3: Grenadier, Londonderry Militia

B

IRISH YEOMANRY, 1798
1: Officer, Eanmenter Cavalry
2 & 3: Privates, Yeomanry infantry

C

BRITISH FENCIBLES, 1798
1: Private, Reay Fencibles
2: Private, Fraser Fencibles
3: Grenadier, Essex Fencibles

D

BRITISH REGULARS; CASTLEBAR, 27 AUGUST 1798
1: Officer, 6th Foot
2: Private, flank company, 6th Foot
3: Trooper, 6th Dragoon Guards (Carabiniers)

E

IRISH INSURGENTS, 1798
1 & 2: Insurgent pikemen, Antrim
3: Insurgent officer, Antrim

F

IRISH INSURGENTS, 1798
1 & 2: Insurgents with firearms
3: Insurgent officer

G

THE FRENCH
1: Chasseur, 3e Chasseurs à Cheval
2: Hussard, 12e Hussards
3: Chasseur, Légion Irlandaise

H

frequently carried the day. There were also a number of occasions – such as the fight at Old Kilcullen – when government cavalrymen re-learned the hard way the old truth that steady pikemen cannot be broken by simply charging straight at them.

Training and leadership

The real problem was the lack of training and militarily-educated leadership. There is evidence of clandestine drilling being carried out in the months before the rebellion, but obviously this could only be done at a local level. Like their Militia counterparts, those involved may have developed a certain level of competence in weapon-handling – learning how to carry and level their pikes in unison, and to stand firmly together – but they had no opportunities to practise co-ordinating the movements of individual companies and regiments. This was evident from the very beginning, and it is worth recounting at a little length the events of 26 May.

The failure of the rebels to launch a co-ordinated assault on Dublin on the night of 24 May can readily be explained by the sudden arrests of the leaders within the capital. Having waited in vain for instructions, the various rebel forces ranged around Dublin simply formed large camps and apparently settled down to await events. Two days later, at the Hill of Tara, Capt Aaron Blanche of the Reay Fencibles won a seemingly impossible victory against overwhelming odds, simply because most of the rebels in one of those camps were no more than passive spectators to their own defeat.

Blanche had originally set out from Dublin in search of a missing baggage party (who had been captured by the rebels), but instead found another detachment of his regiment locked in an argument with some local Yeomanry as to the wisdom of attacking a nearby body of rebels. His colleagues wanted to fall back on Dublin, but by sheer force of personality Blanche took command of the lot, amounting to just 190 men of the Reays and Capt Molloy's Lower Kells Infantry, with a single 6-pdr cannon, and six assorted 'troops' of Yeomanry cavalry amounting to 100 troopers. The rebels were said to be at least 4,000 strong, but despite being outnumbered by more than ten times Blanche and his little band of redcoats set off towards the Hill of Tara.

The rebel position, dominating the Dublin road, was centred on a walled churchyard on the summit of the hill, and extended outwards to take advantage of the ancient earthworks surrounding the hilltop. In the circumstances Blanche took the only possible course open to him, and decided upon an immediate frontal attack, trusting to discipline and the bayonet to carry the day. He drew up his four companies of infantry in a single line, placed half his cavalry on either flank, and then, calling the Yeomanry officers together, 'informed them he had no orders to give, except to lead on their divisions with courage to the action'. As the soldiers advanced up the long grassy slope, the rebels 'put their hats on their pikes, the entire length of the line, and gave three cheers'. However, only a few scattered groups launched unco-ordinated and unsuccessful little rushes

In the virtual absence of reliable images from life of the Irish rebels, a probably more useful illustrator of everyday clothing among the working classes – and one whose work is more nearly contemporary to the '98 – was William Pyne (1769–1843). While the Sun Insurance Company badge and leather helmet worn by this English fireman can be disregarded, the rest of the figure provides a good impression of the sort of sturdy outdoor garments common to farmers and wildfowlers, such as the well-known Shelmalier Marksmen. Note the short, heavy coat, the double-breasted waistcoat, and particularly the turned-down boots worn over thick stockings drawn up over the knee.

William Pyne's study of a baker shows a typical small tradesman's dress of the very early 19th century. Ignore the apron, and probably the stovepipe hat (this taller version of the 'round hat' was only just beginning to appear at the cutting edge of fashion in the mid-1790s); but otherwise, many Irish townsmen would have worn something like this short grey coat cut straight across the waist over a red double-breasted waistcoat, brown knee-breeches, and grey stockings with low shoes.

against the Highlanders, while the rest remained behind the walls and banks. 'On approaching the churchyard gate,' Blanche reported, 'we met with the most obstinate resistance… At one period the King's troops did not gain the least advantage, and finding the men's ammunition almost expended, and our situation getting still more critical, I found it absolutely necessary to make one decisive effort by charging the rebels, which was gallantly executed by the Grenadiers.'

The rush headed by the Reays' grenadier company got them into the walled churchyard, but when they disappeared inside the 6-pdr was left outside, and Capt Molloy himself had to put his hand to the wheel to get it up onto the road. Seeing him struggling, a party of rebels immediately rushed forward, and one supposedly actually touched the barrel before, as Blanche dryly remarked, Molloy 'returned their cordial invitation, which crowned our operations with a complete victory'. The gun's first discharge at murderously close range killed or wounded ten or 12 insurgents; then, while Blanche and his Highlanders plied their bayonets inside the churchyard, Molloy sent round after round of canister into the packed ranks of rebels milling about outside. After a few minutes of this the insurgents started giving way, and, with no proper leaders to rally them, the whole rebel line swiftly crumbled outwards from the centre. Blanche claimed next morning to have counted no fewer than 350 rebel dead, together with immense quantities of arms – as well as recovering his missing baggage party.

Inherent weaknesses

This relatively minor action is recounted in some detail because it encapsulates perfectly the single greatest weakness of the rebel armies. The United Irishmen were primarily a mass political movement, with those taking its oath being automatically enrolled into regiments for a projected army. Despite their obvious disappointment over the French fiasco in Bantry Bay, the United Irish executive reckoned that by February 1798 this army amounted to the impressive figure of 279,896 armed men – on paper. The actual organization was deceptively simple: the United men in each parish formed a company, the companies in each barony a regiment, and the regiments in each county a division, or even an army, depending upon size. For instance, at the beginning of June 1798 Henry Joy McCracken assembled 25 Antrim regiments totalling approximately 12,000 men, which would imply a manageable 500 or so apiece. But although this organization was perfectly adequate for administering a political movement, it did not automatically translate into an effective battlefield organization.

The most important reason was a complete lack of any worthwhile military experience. Those Catholics who had joined the Irish Brigade in French service were essentially conservative, and therefore belonged at the opposite end of the political spectrum from the radical United Irishmen. Thus, with the exception of Lord Edward Fitzgerald – who had briefly served with the British Army in North America – none of those originally elected or appointed as leaders by the County Directories were versed, let alone experienced, in military matters, and in any case the wide-ranging series of arrests in the months leading up to the rebellion saw many of them imprisoned or forced to flee. Some of those who quickly replaced them were men whose sole qualification was bravery and revolutionary fervour; others – such as Bagenal Harvey in Wexford – were intellectual idealists who had no real desire to lead what all too often resembled a terrifying *jacquerie,* more interested in plunder than in the establishment of a democratic republic. Individual commanders – such as McCracken, Munro, and the Wexford priest Father Murphy – were undoubtedly charismatic figures, but even when they took the initiative they invariably lacked a proper staff capable of translating their leadership into co-ordinated action. In the Antrim army the officers were supposedly identified by green cockades, while the rank and file had green hatbands rather than the white ones commonly worn in Wexford, but otherwise there was little to indicate what authority a man might have over those who did not personally recognize him – especially if he was a last-minute replacement.

This practical weakness in command and control was complicated by a variety of other factors. In many rural areas a significant number of officers and men already belonged to an earlier clandestine group known as the 'Defenders'. As their name suggests, this loose collection of rural terrorist groups acted to defend the Catholic peasantry from oppressive landlords; latterly they also engaged in a bitter sectarian struggle against similar groups formed in response by Protestant farmers, such as the equally notorious 'Peep o' Day Boys'. The Defenders were rarely well integrated with the rest of the United movement, preferring to retain their independence rather than recognize the already precarious authority of the United leaders. In the North this problem was exacerbated by the religious divide, since the United Irish movement there was actually founded amongst the politically aware Ulster Scots Presbyterians. Despite their leaders' best efforts to reach out to the Catholic community, many of the local Defenders held back from joining them, fearing (or claiming to fear) that the United men had a secret agenda to create a Presbyterian state.

Moreover, once the risings actually began the rebel armies were joined by all manner of individuals and groups who had not previously been members of the United Irishmen. Some did so out of conviction, some from a sense of adventure, but others – inevitably – were mere opportunists, eager to share in the looting but less keen on fighting.

Insurgent musketeer – a detail from Cruikshank's illustration of Father Murphy and his followers in Wexford. The crested helmet is presumably a captured Yeomanry item, but similar French helmets were issued to Humbert's short-lived *Légion Irlandaise* raised in Co. Mayo.

The massacre of government prisoners and loyalist citizens on Wexford Bridge, 20 June, as depicted by Cruikshank. The flag in the background is described in a contemporary account, but the reconstruction is dubious. In revenge for this atrocity, after Wexford was retaken a few days later captured United Irish leaders, including Father Philip Roche, were hanged on the bridge.

Perhaps most centrally, once the leaders had assembled their formidable numbers of men and brought them to the agreed rendezvous, they then had absolutely no idea what to do with them, except to hurl them at the enemy and hope for the best. The original planning had envisaged that they would simply be assisting a French army of liberation, not that they would be sustaining the fight by themselves – let alone in the absence of orders from a National Directory that had either been arrested or had fled.

THE FRENCH

The French contribution to the campaign was just as haphazard and ultimately as ineffectual. To the French government, Ireland offered an opportunity to knock Britain out of the war, and even if ultimately unsuccessful such an expedition would seriously disrupt British troop deployments overseas (which customarily used the port of Cork as a staging post, particularly for the West Indies).

The campaigns in Germany and Italy took first priority, but late in 1796 Gen Lazare Hoche was authorized to assemble an Armée des Côtes de l'Ocean at Brest. Both the size and actual composition of this force is unclear. The latest in a series of reorganizations at the beginning of the year should have given each *demi-brigade* three battalions, comprising nine companies apiece, and theoretically totalling some 3,000 officers and men, but in fact this was rarely achieved. The regular infantry available to Hoche comprised the 10e, 13e, 52e, 81e and 94e Demi-Brigades d'Infanterie and the 13e Demi-Brigade d'Infanterie Légère. However, as French practice was normally to embark only the second battalion of any regiment selected for such hazardous adventures, this would have given Hoche no more than 6,000 infantry, besides whatever cavalry and artillery could be found. This was clearly going to be inadequate, and he soon set about looking for more.

A Légion Irlandaise had rather hopefully been formed (see Plate A3), but never amounted to anything; so one of Hoche's subordinates, Gen Joseph Humbert, was given the job of creating the Légion des Francs ('Independent Legion') by first skimming 20 men from each battalion in the Armée du Nord. Naturally enough, although he had optimistically asked for their best men, what he got was all the '*rude lapins*' or 'rough rabbits' whom their colonels were only too glad to get rid of. In the end, Humbert also had to accept some '600 *galériens élite*' (special convicts) to complete the Legion, which also became the receptacle for all manner of other waifs and strays.

Unsurprisingly, this Independent Legion – unlike the French regulars – seems to have been regarded as expendable, and when it became clear that the French admiral was unwilling to land any troops in Bantry Bay, the Irish revolutionary Wolfe Tone proposed that

An unsympathetic depiction by Cruikshank of Father John Murphy, one of the rebel leaders in Wexford, with his flag. Note the hooked pike carried by the man behind the priest.

he should be given 'the Légion des Francs, a company of the Artillerie légère, and as many officers as desired to come volunteers in the expedition, with what arms and stores remained, which are now reduced by our separation, to four field-pieces, 20,000 fire-locks at most, 1,000 pounds of powder, and 3,000,000 of cartridges, and to land us in Sligo Bay, and let us make the best of our way, &c... He knew what kind of desperadoes it was composed of and for what purpose; consequently, in the worst event, the republic would be well rid of them.'

On this occasion Tone was turned down, and nearly 400 of the Legion were subsequently lost in the wreck of the *Droits d'homme;* but the expendable nature of the Legion is emphasized by its employment on the Fishguard expedition the following year, and its allocation for an even more abortive descent planned against Newcastle upon Tyne.

Notwithstanding the ignominious failure of the 1796 Bantry Bay expedition, Irish planning was still based upon the arrival of a French army; but it was made clear to the United leaders from the outset that it would not be possible to mount another expedition until August 1798.

General Jean Joseph Aimable Humbert, the French commander of the expeditionary force in 1798, had a colourful later career. As a political opponent of Napoleon Bonaparte he found it prudent to emigrate to America, but fought the British once again at New Orleans in 1815.

This time 3,000 men were to be embarked from Brest and 1,000 from Rochefort, with a further 4,000 to follow, but in the event the expedition never properly got off the ground. The Brest contingent encountered a succession of bureaucratic delays that prevented its sailing until September, leaving the Rochefort contingent on its own.

On 6 August, Gen Humbert, having survived the wreck of the *Droits d'homme* in 1796, sailed from that port with a total of just 1,019 men, which according to Col Sarrazin included:

Staff: 35 officers
2e Bataillon/70e Demi-Brigade de Ligne – 38 officers, 794 men
Compagnie de grenadiers francs, 108e/109e DBs – 2 officers, 51 men
Détachement, 11e Compagnie de Canonniers de la 12e Division – 2 officers, 40 men
Détachement, 3e Chasseurs à Cheval – 3 officers, 43 men
Détachement,12e Hussards – 11 men serving as Gen Humbert's escort.

Of these, both the men of 2/70e Demi-Brigade and the independent grenadier company drawn from the 108e and 109e Demi-Brigades were veterans; the 2/70e came from the Army of Italy, and the 108e/109e from Germany. While the 3e Chasseurs à Cheval afterwards claimed Castlebar as one of their *combats*, it would appear that only the 11 troopers of the 12e Hussards who formed the French general's personal escort were actually mounted there; Sarazin describes the decisive 'cavalry charge' at Castlebar as having being made by Humbert himself at the head of his staff.

In addition to the regulars, Sarrazin also mentions a 40-strong contingent of Irish volunteers who were intended to serve as the cadre for a new Légion Irlandaise hastily raised in Co. Mayo after Humbert's arrival, and organized, clothed and equipped as a French auxiliary unit – albeit a very uncertain one (see Plate H3).

PLATE COMMENTARIES

A: THE LAST IRISH BRIGADES

A1: Officer, Dillon's Regiment, 1794
Barred by their religion from service in the British Army, the Irish Catholic gentry had traditionally soldiered abroad, usually as 'Wild Geese' in the French Army's Irish Brigade. During the Seven Years' War that brigade boasted a cavalry regiment and six infantry regiments (besides two Scottish emigré regiments who were also accounted a part of it). However, by the late 18th century they had been consolidated into only three regiments, albeit now with two battalions apiece – the Régiments Dillon, Berwick and Walsh.

In 1791 all three were officially redesignated simply as the 87e, 88e and 92e Régiments d'Infanterie respectively; however, they still had Irish or Franco-Irish officers. At the instigation of a prominent colonial planter named Victor Martin O'Gorman, the second battalions of all three regiments

were ordered to San Domingo in November 1791, in order to help suppress the growing slave revolt that would eventually result in the creation of the black Empire of Haiti. Instead, after a difficult voyage exacerbated by unrest in the ranks, they were badly defeated in a battle at Les Plantons, and could do nothing to avert the colony's downward spiral into anarchy. The result was that when a small British force arrived off the St Nicholas Mole in September 1793, the remaining 180 men of the Régiment Dillon led by Maj Denis O'Farrell not only surrendered on the spot, but promptly changed sides.

Early British Army returns initially referred to the unit as the 2/87e, but it quickly reverted to its original designation as Dillon's Regiment. In July 1794, Col Whitelocke, the British commander at the Mole, was grumbling that 'Dillon's Regiment certainly requires reform and the introduction of a class of officers different from those of which it is now composed. Most of them have been brought from the Ranks and appointed by Major O'Farrel, more to prevent their being mischievous than as a reward for any merit they possess.' This is probably something of an exaggeration (Denis O'Farrell himself had entered the regiment as a *sous-lieutenant* as long ago as 1777). Notwithstanding Whitelocke's poor opinion, the regiment fought well at St Marc in September, standing 'firm as a rock' to repulse a Republican assault. Nevertheless, 12 months later there were just 18 officers, 16 sergeants, 11 drummers and 68 men remaining, and with no realistic hope of maintaining the regiment it was disbanded late the following year. The survivors were seemingly absorbed into an entirely new Dillon's Regiment.

This reconstruction is largely based on a contemporary silhouette of another long-serving officer on San Domingo, Capt Plunckett, who was first commissioned in 1784. When the old regimental titles were supposedly abolished in favour of French Line numbers in 1791, all three of the Irish regiments were officially allocated black facings; but there was no opportunity (or desire) to alter their uniforms before they embarked for the Caribbean, and Dillon retained its yellow facings to the end. Interestingly, while Plunckett is otherwise still dressed as a French officer, with no sash and his sword belt worn under his waistcoat, his coat lapels are loosely buttoned back in the British fashion. His only concession to the climate appears to be his broad-brimmed hat.

A2: Officer, 4th Battalion (Daniel O'Connell's), Irish Brigade, 1796

Nothing more is known of the survivors of Walsh's Regiment on San Domingo, although some men of Berwick, having gone over to the Republicans, were reported to have headed an assault on a British outpost as late as 1795. In Europe it was a similar story; in 1792 the first battalions of the three regiments in French service officially lost their foreign status entirely, and were ordered to adopt white uniforms in conformity with the rest of the infantry. Instead, when the Bourbon princes attempted to rally what remained of the French royal army most of 1/Berwick defected to join them. Together with the equivalent of reinforced companies from 1/Dillon and 1/Walsh, they re-formed a small Brigade Irlandaise, only to be disbanded in October of that year. Even that, however, was not the end of the brigade.

In April 1794 the Westminster Parliament passed an act 'to enable subjects of France to enlist as soldiers' in the British Army, and to receive commissions – irrespective of their religion. As originally conceived, this measure was intended to permit the formation of French Royalist émigré units under direct British control; but it also paved the way for the resurrection of the Irish Brigade. On 1 October 1794, no fewer than six battalions were authorized.[2] The Hon Henry Dillon's 3/Irish Brigade went to San Domingo in March 1796, and there absorbed what remained of the original Régiment Dillon. While the experiment was successful enough in itself, it was soon realized that the removal of the bar on recruiting and commissioning Roman Catholics meant that there was no reason why they should not be channelled into ordinary regiments of the British Line rather than forming discrete Catholic corps, and so the last Irish Brigade was finally disbanded early in 1798.

This reconstruction is based upon two miniature portraits, of Col Count Daniel O'Connell of 4/Irish Brigade and Capt Maurice Charles O'Connell of the same unit. Both reveal a scarlet coat with sky-blue collar, cuffs and lapels, with

Captain John Clayton Cowell of 1st Battalion, 1st (Royal) Regiment, after the painting by William Beechey. The painting was made some time between Cowell's return from San Domingo in late 1794, and his brevet promotion to major on 1 January 1798 – the sword appears to be the 1796 pattern.

silver-laced buttonholes set in pairs, silver epaulettes embroidered with an Irish harp, and facing-colour turnbacks in French style rather than the white normally worn in the British service. Details of the uniforms worn by the other five battalions are unrecorded, but on the evidence of its surviving colours the Hon Henry Dillon's 3/Irish Brigade must have had yellow facings, just like their predecessors in the French service; if they were consciously duplicating the original uniform, it is also likely that the collar may have been red rather than yellow, as worn when in the French service. Similarly, it may also reasonably be inferred that the Duc de Fitzjames' 1/Irish Brigade had the black facings of the old Régiment Berwick, while Count Walsh-Serrant's 2/Irish Brigade had the dark blue facings of the original Régiment Walsh. A surviving breastplate (belt plate), probably belonging to Dillon's since it is associated with the colours, bears a Garter strap with the inscription LOYAL IRISH BRIGADE, surmounted by a crown. The centre is now blank, but presumably was intended to bear the number '3'; the example depicted in Capt Charles O'Connell's portrait appears to have the same device with a prominent number '4' in the centre.

---

2 For service histories, see MAA 328: *Émigré and Foreign Troops in British Service (1): 1793–1802*.

A3: Officer, Légion Irlandaise, 1796

In France, meanwhile, what was left of the original Brigade Irlandaise after the various defections and desertions disappeared entirely in the amalgamations of 1794 and 1795. These split up the individual battalions of the old regular regiments to form the nuclei of *demi-brigades de bataille*, which were otherwise formed of volunteers and new conscripts, and bore entirely new numbers. None of the new units were built around the 'Irish' battalions, and their numbers 87e, 88e and 92e were eventually given to completely unrelated formations.

However, in 1796 a new Légion Irlandaise was authorized, to form part of Gen Hoche's expeditionary force to Ireland. No longer formed of émigré Catholics, this new Irish Legion was not a revival of the old one, but was to be raised by political radicals directly linked to the United Irishmen and committed to establishing a revolutionary Irish Republic. Nevertheless, perhaps predictably, they were dressed (or at least intended to be dressed) in red coats cut in light infantry style and faced with green, as depicted here after Richard Knötel. Since the other auxiliary battalions being raised for Hoche's expedition had to make do with an assortment of whatever clothing and equipment could be scavenged from the depots, including captured British uniforms hastily dyed and re-cut in light infantry style, there is room for doubt as to whether the rank and file were ever as well dressed as this lieutenant.

At any rate, the projected two battalions only ever amounted to a handful of officers and men, most of whom were soon absorbed into another of Hoche's units, the brown-coated Légion des Francs. Only some 40 of them remained long enough to eventually accompany Humbert's force to Killala in August 1798, and to act as the cadre for a locally raised force that would also take the title Légion Irlandaise (see Plate H3). After that last débâcle the survivors were formally disbanded on 21 February 1799; they had no direct connection with Napoleon's Légion Irlandaise, raised in 1803.

B: IRISH MILITIA, 1798

Thomas Robinson's well-known contemporary painting of the battle of Ballynahinch reveals that in June 1798, at least, some of the Irish Militia were still wearing pre-1796 pattern coats – long and swallow-tailed, and cut away in front to expose the waistcoat – rather than the new, shorter style closed to the waist.

B1: Sergeant-Major, Antrim Militia

Like most of the Irish garrison, the Antrim Militia were scattered across the countryside in small detachments, and in the first few days of the rebellion they found themselves fighting a desperate series of actions against far larger bodies of rebels. Lieutenant Gardner's defence of Baltinglas on 25 May, with just 50 of his own men and a number of small Yeomanry units, was typical. As the *Gentleman's Magazine* reported at the time:

'He at first took an advantageous situation in front of the town; but after a few shots without effect, the rebels filed off in every direction to surround him. He then retreated into the town to defend the barracks. A contest took place in the midst of the flames for near 9 hours, for the rebels set fire to the town. They were at last repulsed with considerable loss; many dead were found in the streets and ditches, and 30 cartloads of killed and wounded were carried off in their retreat. Captain Hardy, of the Hacketstown yeoman infantry, fell early in the action. His other loss consists of 10 privates killed, and 1 serjeant and 19 privates wounded.' Subsequently other detachments of the regiment were caught up in the debacle at Three Rocks; took part in the desperate defence of New Ross; and 'acted in the most spirited and determined manner' in the battle of Arklow on 9 June 1798.

The print by Bunbury on which this figure is partly based is simply labelled as a sergeant of infantry, but is more properly a sergeant-major, being identified as such by his epaulette, sash, curved sword, and perhaps above all by his smart and soldier-like appearance. Yellow was the most popular facing colour adopted by Irish Militia units, being worn by nearly half of them – 17 out of the total of 38 corps.

B2: Private, flank company, Monaghan Militia

Taken directly from Robinson's painting, the subject is identified as a member of a flank company by the white-fringed wings on his shoulders. His white-faced coatee is of the pre-1796 pattern; here his cartridge box hides the 'vertical' pockets with four paired, square-ended lace loops shown by Robinson. His mitre-like cap, probably of leather and trimmed with wool 'feathers', was a fairly popular style among British Army light infantry in the late 18th century. While the details of the various cap fronts depicted in the painting are unclear, at least one man can be seen to wear the traditional light infantry bugle-horn badge, and another appears to have a grenade badge instead. The figure on which this reconstruction is based has a white waistcoat rather than the red one normally worn by light infantry at this period. It may simply be a lightweight summer garment, like the white linen gaiter trousers also shown as being worn by this and other militia units; but it is equally possible that he is a grenadier, and that the grenadier company wore these caps in preference to the traditional but more expensive fur cap.

B3: Grenadier, Londonderry Militia

There is no ambiguity about the status of this bearskin-capped grenadier of Lord Castlereagh's Londonderry Militia. When fur caps were officially introduced into the British Army in 1768 they at first followed the same profile as the old cloth mitre caps, inclining slightly forward to terminate in a noticeable point. However, by the end of the century a variety of near-cylindrical, almost flat-topped shapes can be seen in a number of illustrations of regular, Militia and Volunteer units. This particular pattern appears to have been a common one; more familiarly shown in a contemporary print of a soldier of the East Yorkshire Militia, it also appears being worn by a company of soldiers in a contemporary illustration supposedly depicting Lake's victory at Vinegar Hill (though other figures are evidently based on contemporary images of the Footguards light companies, and the Irish insurgents are all depicted wearing French uniforms). The coat is the old swallow-tailed pattern, with tufted shoulder straps worn above the flank-company wings. Note the old-fashioned belly-box with additional cartridges (also worn by B2); the grenade badge above the plate on his bayonet belt; and the tower motif on his knapsack.

C: IRISH YEOMANRY, 1798

When the Yeomanry corps were first authorized there appears to have been a popular perception that they could

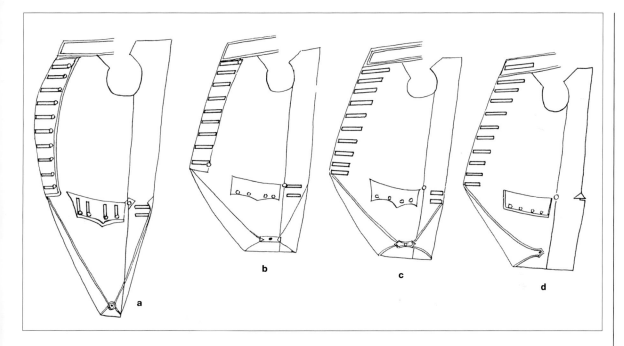

b

a

c

d

dress pretty much as they pleased, but the government – with unhappy memories of the earlier, free-thinking Volunteer movement – had definite ideas on this point. Consequently, the overwhelming majority of units wore red, and while the physical evidence of their appearance is far from abundant, it does indicate a similar consistency in style to that displayed by Volunteer units on the mainland.

C1: Officer, Eanmenter Cavalry

This figure is largely reconstructed around a surviving jacket and waistcoat worn by Capt Richard D'Arcy of this County Galway corps. The fairly loose cut of the jacket is very similar to those then being worn by regular light dragoons, as illustrated in Le Marchant's *Sword Exercise*, with the obvious difference that the three rows of buttons on the front are not linked by decorative cords, probably for reasons of economy. Very similar jackets with dark blue collar and cuffs are also illustrated in Robinson's painting of Ballynahinch (possibly worn by the Belfast Yeomanry Cavalry), and in a painting of an officer of the Cork Yeomanry. Similar jackets in red also found favour with Scottish and English Fencible and Yeomanry units, and blue ones, although rare, were not unknown (Robinson's painting also depicts some unidentified troopers in blue jackets faced and lined with red.) Otherwise, the ubiquitous fur-crested Tarleton helmet, breeches, boots and accoutrements are the same as those worn by regulars, with the exception that some units did not receive carbines until after the rising had commenced.

C2 & C3: Privates, Yeomanry infantry

Reliable information on the uniforms worn by the numerous infantry corps raised as part of the Irish Yeomanry is almost entirely lacking, and the two soldiers depicted here are therefore substantially based on Thomas Rowlandson's exactly contemporary illustrations of their counterparts in the various London Volunteer corps.

Evolution of British soldiers' coats in the 1790s, in images based on a notebook associated with the London clothier J. N. & B. Pearse. (a) The 'Old Pattern', cut swallow-tail fashion, exposing the waistcoat. (b) The 'New Fashion' of June 1796, with the coat effectively cropped as a jacket, and cut with the front hooking together all the way from the throat to the waist. (c) The 'New Regulation Fashion' of 1798, following the abolition of lapels on 28 October 1797. (d) The final jacket is the 1799 pattern with the rear turn-back abolished. This style was already being worn In 1798 by light infantry, albeit with the false pockets placed vertically rather than horizontally as shown here.

Some Yeomanry infantry units may have worn military cocked hats, but it seems likely that they mostly followed their mainland counterparts in adopting the much more stylish Tarleton helmet (C2), or the cheaper alternative of a 'round hat' with a fur crest (C3). One of the officers grouped around the dying Capt Evatt in Thomas Robinson's painting of Ballynahinch certainly wears a round hat, although another and more senior officer with the same yellowish buff facings has an ordinary cocked hat. While otherwise unidentified, they presumably represent one of the local Yeomanry corps rather than the Fife Fencibles who were also present; they are most likely from the Seaforde Infantry, who were the only Yeomanry infantry corps to return any casualties in that battle.

As with the Militia, the old pre-1796 swallow-tailed coat may have still prevailed; London Volunteer corps were certainly wearing them until at least 1803 – perhaps because, being part-timers, they had no need to renew their clothing annually. It is possible, however, that short single-breasted jackets were adopted by some newly-raised units for the sake of economy. Facing colours are again largely a matter for conjecture, although the Belfast Yeomanry certainly had black. On the scanty evidence available, dark blue may have been the most popular choice, although instances of yellow facings are also recorded.

As with their mounted colleagues, the arms and accoutrements provided were largely the same as for regulars and Militia, with the important difference that as part-timers intended to serve in their own districts there is no evidence that they were equipped with knapsacks, or received from the Ordnance stores camp equipage such as canteens and haversacks. Consequently, the two Yeomen depicted here have been forced to improvise with blankets or civilian greatcoats rolled on their backs.

D: BRITISH FENCIBLES, 1798

D1: Private, Reay Fencibles

The Reays, raised in the north of Scotland by Mackay Hugh Baillie of Rosehall late in 1794, were probably the most famous of the 'Scotch Fencibles' employed in place of regulars in the Irish garrison. At the outset of the rebellion a detachment of three companies, supported by men of the Upper Kells Cavalry and Lower Kells Infantry, routed a much larger rebel force at the Hill of Tara. The unit served very creditably throughout the rebellion, and took part in the final battle outside Killala. Their colours, bearing a curious crowned thistle-star device (as just visible on the knapsack, left background) may still be seen in Edinburgh Castle. Thanks to the survival of the regimental orderly book, their uniform can be reconstructed with some confidence.

In most Highland corps the bonnet was ornamented ('mounted') with ostrich feathers, but references in regimental orders suggests that the Reay Fencibles adopted a piece of bearskin, probably on grounds of cost. For most duties the men wore the 'hummle' (humble) bonnet devoid of any embellishment, while officers sported round hats. The jacket was of scarlet cloth for officers and sergeants, and red for the rank and file. Prior to 1797 it was worn open in front, displaying the white waistcoat underneath. This soldier, however, is wearing the 1796-pattern coatee, cut in the light infantry style that was customary for Highland regiments, and now fastened with hooks-and-eyes all the way down the front rather than at the throat alone. Collar, cuffs and lapels are in the regiment's greyish-blue facings, with buttons and loops. The lace was silver with a blue thread in the centre for officers, and of white braid with the usual coloured worm for the men, although the precise pattern is unknown. Officers had two small flat epaulettes of silver bullion with a fringe, a blue binding round the edge, and two stripes of blue silk along the centre of the strap; they were ornamented with a gold-embroidered thistle for the battalion companies, and a grenade and bugle-horn respectively for the flank companies. The waistcoats were of white cassimere or cloth, plain, and fastened by a single row of small regimental buttons.

Unless the belted plaid in Mackay tartan, as seen here, was specifically ordered, the men wore the *feilebeag* or 'little kilt'. According to regimental orders the amount of tartan allowed for making up the little kilt was 3½ yards for the grenadier company and 3 yards for the other companies. Purses or sporrans were only worn in review order. Those of officers and sergeants were of badger-skin, with the head of the animal closing the mouth (as later worn by the Argyll & Sutherland Highlanders), surmounted by a straight silver rim, and ornamented with six white goat-hair tassels of 'shaving-

'Sergeant of infantry' – a print by Bunbury, in fact depicting a more senior non-commissioned officer (see Plate B1). This old style of uniform was officially superseded for regular units in January 1796, but, apart from the gaiters reaching above the knee, it was still seen worn by Militia and Yeomanry in 1798.

brush' pattern mounted in silver or white-metal bells. The purses of the rank and file were of white goatskin, with a plain straight white-metal top, and six short black horse-hair tassels in metal bells.

In practice, officers generally wore white breeches and Hessian boots on parade; for undress, they had grey pantaloons with hussar or 'half-boots', and for fatigues or when in camp 'field-dress' they seem to have worn plain jackets or frocks. Similarly, for fatigue wear some of the men had trousers of blue or grey cloth or tartan, but as this garment was not officially recognized in clothing regulations it was acknowledged that 'uniformity was not expected'.

Indeed, it is hard to avoid the impression that there was little effort to conform with regulations at all, and the officers seem to have been particularly resistant to any attempt to force them to wear Highland dress.

D2: Private, Fraser Fencibles

Raised in direct competition with the Reays, the Frasers should have been equally splendidly uniformed when they took the field against the French at Castlebar, for when first recruited they had the black velvet facings so often associated with Inverness-shire regiments, and were to wear 'the usual highland garb with belted plaids, and philbegs [kilts] of Fraser tartan but without broadswords'. Exactly what was understood at this time to be the Fraser tartan is uncertain, but of little consequence, since it appears that the normal order of dress was the grey linen trousers depicted here. The bonnet had a red tourie, like that of the Reays, but was partially mounted with a few black ostrich feathers. The coatee is of the older 1796 cutaway pattern, exposing the white waistcoat.

The Regimental Colour followed the usual pattern for units displaying black facings, having a red St George's cross overall on a black ground, with the Union in the canton. Interestingly, a sketch in the National Army Museum depicts the post-1801 Union with St Patrick's cross included, while the usual wreath in the centre is still the pre-1801 style formed of roses and thistles alone; presumably the existing colours were 'updated' prior to the regiment's disbandment in July 1802, rather than replaced with a new set. The wreath was surmounted at the break by a crown, and in the centre a thistle flower was embroidered in proper colours; below it a white silk scroll bore the title FRASER FENCIBLES embroidered in gold. The King's Colour was presumably similarly decorated, but may have been the one lost at Castlebar.

D3: Grenadier, Essex Fencibles

The Essex Fencibles were based at Ballyshannon during the rising, and their commander, Col James Edward Urquhart, succeeded in keeping the district quiet even after the arrival of the French. Consequently the regiment saw little action, although a detachment took part in Vereker's celebrated stand against the French at Collooney. Fortunately, however, a set of regimental orders survive, which lay down exactly what was to be worn and when.

Officers were to wear scarlet coats faced buff (Jamie Urquhart had originally served in the 14th Foot) with silver embroidered button-holes, buff waistcoats and breeches, silver-laced hats with white feathers, and for the grenadiers a plain black hat with white feather. The light company were to wear jackets rather than coats, with red waistcoats, and had leather caps with green feathers. When on duty, officers were to wear long gaiters, but otherwise could have boots or shoes. In undress the coat had plain buff facings without embroidery, and a plain hat was to be worn. Greatcoats were dark blue with a scarlet collar and cuffs and buff edging; both epaulettes and sword belt were to be worn outside the greatcoat.

The NCOs were similarly dressed. Sergeants also had dark blue greatcoats edged buff, but only the collar was red, while corporals had only plain blue greatcoats. As to the rank and file, grenadiers and light company men were to wear bearskin caps and leather caps respectively when on duty, and the battalion company men hats (as does this grenadier). In wet

Foreground, a flank company man of the Monaghan Militia, in Robinson's painting of Ballynahinch (see Plate B2). His hairstyle seems to identify him as a grenadier; although the badge on his mitre-style cap is unclear, it does not seem to be the light infantry bugle-horn worn on the same cap by the soldier in the background immediately left of the King's Colour. Beside that man is an officer, perhaps of the Seaforde Infantry, wearing a fur-crested 'round hat'.

Captain John Rose of Holm, an officer of the Strathspey Fencibles, as caricatured by John Kay. This particular regiment did not serve in Ireland, but their uniform was virtually identical to that of a number of Highland regiments that did. Most notable is the fact that while the rank and file wore kilts and feathered bonnets, the officers, like those of the Reay Fencibles, normally wore breeches and fur-crested round hats.

weather they were to wear drab-coloured coats over both their uniforms and cross-belts; since these are not referred to as greatcoats, they presumably lacked shoulder capes. Off duty they were allowed foraging caps, half-gaiters and jackets, and on the march white trousers were to be worn. Pioneers were to wear bearskin caps and leather aprons when the regiment was under arms, i.e. on parade, but presumably wore forage caps while working. Drummers and fifers, who wore the usual reversed colours, were to have bearskin caps when on duty, but at all other times wore leather caps with red feathers. Their slightly superior status as the battalion's signallers was also marked by having plain blue greatcoats like the corporals. As an old regular who had fought at Bunker Hill, Urquhart also insisted that the NCOs and drummers were to have their hair dressed and powdered every day, and the latter were always to have theirs turned up under their caps.

E: BRITISH REGULARS; CASTLEBAR, 27 AUGUST 1798

General Lake's forces at Castlebar comprised some 1,700 men, with most belonging to two Irish Militia regiments, from Kilkenny and Longford, and the Galway Yeomanry Infantry. He also had a few cavalry, including a handful of the 6th Dragoon Guards (Carabiniers); but seemingly the only men to be relied upon were the four companies of the Fraser Fencibles, amounting to no more than 150 men, and a single company of 60 men – poignantly described as 'a remnant' – from the regular 6th of Foot.

E1: Officer, 6th Foot

This officer is wearing the new single-breasted jacket prescribed for officers on 28 October 1797. While a very practical-looking garment it appears to have been unpopular, perhaps due to its plainness, and the order was subsequently rescinded on 26 May 1798. Nevertheless, officers in possession of the new jackets were officially permitted to continue wearing them up to 24 December 1798, and unofficially did so for quite some time afterwards. One of William Loftie's watercolours (see opposite) reveals that they were worn by the officers of the 16th Foot on the Surinam expedition; he shows other ranks'-style shoulder straps edged in silver lace. Eventually the jacket re-appeared without tails, as the undress shell jacket. In keeping with the informal style of the jacket this officer has chosen to wear the very popular crested round hat in preference to the regulation cocked one. His gorget and crimson waist sash are the only immediately obvious signs of officer status. In the field he wears a personally acquired canteen and satchel slung over his sword belt.

E2: Private, flank company, 6th Foot

While officers were expected to alter or replace their uniforms at their own expense as soon as a new pattern was promulgated, the clothing for regiments serving in Ireland was to be made there and delivered by 10 June each year, after which it still had to be fitted and altered before issue. In the circumstances, it is extremely unlikely that the 6th Foot received the single-breasted 1798-pattern coatee until after the fighting was over, and they were almost certainly dressed like the private of the Essex Fencibles (D3). However, the 1798 jacket is illustrated here in order to complete the picture of the evolution of the British soldier's clothing in the last decade of the 18th century.

E3: Trooper, 6th Dragoon Guards (Carabiniers)

Quite aside from Dublin Castle's chronic inability to promptly implement instructions from London, it is difficult to be certain as to the style of uniform actually worn by the hapless troopers of the Carabiniers at Castlebar. In theory the various alterations in the infantry uniform, including the removal of lapels, ought to have been paralleled in the heavy cavalry. However, clothing for mounted personnel was only renewed every two years rather than annually as in the infantry. It therefore took quite some time for alterations in style to take effect, and some contemporary illustrations – such as Hamilton Smith's sketches – indicate that the lapels seen here were still being worn by some heavy cavalry as late as 1800.

Otherwise the rest of this unhorsed trooper's clothing and equipment are unremarkable. The bicorne hat was becoming impractically large, and at Den Helder in the following year at least some of the infantry were noted wearing them fore-and-aft in the French style (a practice soon enthusiastically taken up by everyone who could not find an excuse to wear a cap instead). There was a similar time lag when it came to equipment. The regiments of Dragoon Guards and Dragoons were originally armed with a carbine-bore version of the standard infantry musket with a 42in barrel, but in recognition that this was an unnecessary encumbrance when they no longer had a mounted infantry role, a new weapon with a 26in barrel was approved in 1796. However, production of the new carbine did not actually begin until late 1797, and in the meantime regiments were instructed to have the barrels of their 1770-pattern carbines cut down to the new size. The altered weapon carried by this trooper can readily be distinguished from the 1796 pattern by the stock profile and furniture.

F: IRISH INSURGENTS, 1798

F1 & F2: Insurgent pikemen, Antrim

Authentic contemporary images of the Irish rebels are virtually non-existent, and modern reconstructions are generally too reliant on Cruickshank's caricature illustrations from a generation or so later. F1 and F2 are therefore necessarily based on contemporary depictions of typical working men's clothing – in this case, those by William Pyne, of a Smithfield drover and a bill-poster. (Indeed, it is entirely possible that Pyne's drover was in fact an Irishman.) The cropping of the swallow-tailed coat skirts to turn the garment into a jacket was a practical and common practice in both town and country. Pyne's drover was wearing a white jacket, but like his bill-poster both our subjects wear the indeterminate brown shade sometimes referred to as 'country grey'. As with Scottish 'hodden grey' and Confederate 'butternut', this was a woollen material that was dyed grey as part of the finishing process, but when exposed to sunlight rapidly turned brown. So universal was this colour that one British officer complained that Irish Yeomanry and Militia wantonly murdered anyone in a brown coat, on the assumption that if he was a countryman he must also be a rebel. The headgear worn by F2 is a fairly shapeless slouch hat, but F1's 'flowerpot' style is also familiar from Cruickshank's caricatures. Note the green cloth bands worn as field signs; in the Antrim army these were apparently normal, while a Wexford force are described with white hat bands and green cockades (the latter possibly a sign of officer status). Some of Gillray's caricatures also show bunches of green leaves worn on hats.

F3: Insurgent officer, Antrim

While some rebel commanders simply turned out wearing a decent suit of clothes embellished with the obligatory green cockade and a sword of some description, a surprising number were described as wearing 'regimentals' or proper military uniforms. Lord Edward Fitzgerald had apparently intended to wear a specially made hussar-style suit in bottle-green, but the majority were old uniforms from Volunteer days. The green coat depicted here – which survives – is associated with Henry Joy McCracken, but generally red or blue coats predominated. For example, a party of United Irishmen who invaded Baltinglas in search of arms shortly before the rebellion were reported to

Officer of the 16th Foot in Surinam, 1804, after William Loftie. This sketch is chiefly interesting in depicting the single-breasted 1797-pattern jacket supposedly phased out in 1798 (see Plate E1).

have been led by men in blue regimentals turned up with red. One oddity was the rebel commander at the Hill of Tara; said to be the son of a local innkeeper and a deserter from the Kildare Militia, he wore a white uniform, so was popularly believed to be a French officer. While at first sight unlikely, there may actually be an element of truth in the story; the last of the old Brigade Irlandaise were ordered to exchange their red coats for white ones faced with blue on being absorbed into the French Line.

G: IRISH INSURGENTS, 1798

G1 & G2: Insurgents with firearms

Once again, Pyne's costume sketches form the basis for our reconstructions, this time of the more 'middling' class of rebel. As the insurgents rested in the shade of some woods before the battle of Ballynahinch, a 12-year-old boy named James Thomson observed their appearance:

They wore no uniforms; yet they presented a tolerably decent appearance being dressed, no doubt, in their 'Sunday clothes'… The only thing in which they all concurred was the wearing of green: almost every individual having a knot of ribbons of that colour, sometimes mixed with yellow, in his hat … and many … bore ornaments of various descriptions and of different degrees of taste and

A Smithfield drover, as depicted by William Pyne – a useful print illustrating a common style of working clothing of the period, as worn in Ireland as well as England. The tall-crowned hat is the basis of the narrower-brimmed 'flowerpot' style shown by Cruikshank. Note the practical and widespread habit of cropping the coat skirts to jacket length. Between the brown knee-breeches and the white stockings, a flash of red suggests a second pair of lighter stockings worn beneath. Note the side-buttoned ankle boots.

Another of Pyne's tradesmen, again showing a cut of clothing relevant to Plates F and G; here he illustrates a bill-poster with a glue can, short apron and long brush. Cruickshank shows 'flowerpot' hats in all his illustrations of Irish rebels, but Gillray shows broader-brimmed slouches with the brims folded in various ways. Here the hat is grey, the neck cloth pink, the shirt white, the waistcoat light blue-grey, the uncropped coat brown with cloth-covered buttons, the trousers faded red, and the battered ankle boots black, over white stockings.

execution; the most of which had been presented as tributes of regard and affection and as incentives to heroic deeds, by females whose breasts beat as high in patriotic ardour as those of their husbands, their sweethearts and their brothers....

Both men have captured weapons and accoutrements. At Clane, on the first night of the uprising, Richard Griffith of the Sallins Yeomanry found himself under attack by a band of rebels who had just massacred the nearby garrison at Prosperous: 'The party made a very formidable appearance,' he confessed, 'not so much from its numbers, though very considerable, but from the brightness of the Arms, the Scarlet Coats, Helmets, etc.' Some of the red coats were worn by former members of the Yeomanry turned rebel, but others may have been stripped from the bodies of their victims; Griffith's narrative continued: 'I charged them with my sixteen yeomen and cut down several rascals whose heads were ornamented with Ancient Briton's Helmets, Cork Militia Hats etc.'

G1, based on Pyne's baker and a Cruickshank illustration, is a respectably dressed man sporting a knot of yellow and green ribbons on his hat, who has acquired a set of Militia or Yeomanry infantry accoutrements. **G2**, based loosely on both Pyne's rendering of a London fireman and more closely on one of Gillray's subjects, has a Yeomanry helmet and a cavalry sling belt, with the cartridge pouch pulled round toward the front to be more accessible.

G3: Insurgent officer

This figure is a composite of two contemporary illustrations; one is a pencil sketch of an unknown rebel wearing a greatcoat, 'who threatened to murder Mrs Tighe', and the other a depiction of a grocer turned rebel colonel named McCulloch, in Robinson's painting of Ballynahinch (see page 19). Beneath a caped greatcoat he wears a brown jacket with a red stand-and-fall collar and cloth-covered buttons, paler brown knee breeches, and stockings. We have given him a captured cavalry sabre and belt.

H: THE FRENCH

The greater part of Gen Humbert's small French force was made up of ordinary infantry of the Line, dressed in the 'national' uniform of long-tailed blue coats with white facings and red trim, white waistcoats and breeches or trousers, and black cocked hats. There were also some gunners in their traditional all-blue uniform with red trim, and a few cavalrymen to lend a brave touch of colour.

H1: Chasseur, 3e Chasseurs à Cheval

This trooper has laid aside his equipment while he tries to impart the rudiments of musketry to one of the Irish volunteers recruited at Killala. He still wears the hussar-style uniform adopted in the 1790s, at first with an imitation-fur crested casque, and then with the hussar mirliton depicted here. Unlike hussars, however, the chasseurs' braided and corded dolman was normally worn open to reveal the waistcoat, and a barrelled sash was not worn. Regimental facing colours were allocated in groups of three; in this case, 1e Chasseurs had red collar and cuffs, 2e Chasseurs green collars and red cuffs, and 3e Chasseurs red collars but green cuffs. On active service, as depicted here, green overalls were worn, but dress uniform included tight green pantaloons with hussar-style braiding.

H2: Hussard, 12e Hussards

Apart from their brief moment of glory at Castlebar, Ireland was an unlucky place for the 12e Hussards, who had originally been raised as the Hussards de la Montagne in 1793. Two squadrons of the regiment were captured at sea during Hoche's disastrous expedition to Bantry Bay in 1796, and were held as prisoners for two years before being exchanged.

During its comparatively short existence the regiment underwent a confusing series of changes to its uniform. As originally raised, the Hussards de la Montagne appear to have had an all-brown uniform, but following their amalgamation with other volunteer units on 9 February 1794, and redesignation as 12e Hussards, the brown dolman and pelisse were retained but red breeches were adopted, as depicted here. When the regiment was rebuilt in 1799 after the Irish debacle an almost completely new uniform was prescribed: the brown dolman now had light blue facings, and the pelisse, breeches, and the *flamme* on the cap also became light blue; one source gives red boots, although this may have been an affectation confined to the officers. In 1803 the regiment was redesignated yet again, taking the altogether less dashing identity and role of the 30e Dragons.

H3: Chasseur, Légion Irlandaise

The extravagant allowance of 35 staff officers recorded by Col Sarrazin was presumably intended to administer the large numbers of Irish insurgents confidently expected to flock to meet the expedition on its arrival, and in addition there were also *'une quarantaine d'Irlandais servant dans nos rangs, destinés à encadre les Irlandais'* – 'about 40 Irishmen serving in our ranks, intended to provide a cadre for the Irish [volunteers].' Sarrazin also added that this cadre had agreed to be paid and fed as ordinary soldiers. They were presumably the last remaining personnel of the Légion Irlandaise formed optimistically two years earlier (see Plate A3), and upon landing in Ireland they did indeed help to form a French-sponsored unit bearing that title. Alas, despite being raised as an auxiliary corps of the French Army, and despite their French uniforms, the Légion Irlandaise were always regarded by the British Army simply as rebels and denied the status of legitimate combatants. Their former French masters seem to have stood aside without protest while they were hunted down and slaughtered after Ballinamuck and Killala.

Surprisingly enough, providing them with uniforms was one of the first things Humbert did when he rounded up recruits for the unit at Killala. The Légion Irlandaise were apparently dressed in the scourings of the Rochefort arsenal, which, as Bishop Stock recalled, included a supply of obsolete infantry helmets:

The coxcombry of the young clowns in their new dress; the mixture of good humour and contempt in the countenances of the French, employed in making puppies of them; the haste of the undressed to be as fine as their neighbours, casting away their old clothes long before it came their turn to receive the new; above all, the merry activity of a handsome young fellow, a marine officer, whose business it was to consummate the vanity of the recruits by decorating them with helmets beautifully edged with spotted brown paper to look like leopard's skin, a task which he performed standing on a powder barrel, and making the helmet fit any skull, even the largest, by thumping it down with his fists, careless whether it could ever be taken off again...

There is no mention of the red coats prescribed for the original Légion Irlandaise, and instead this recruit has been issued with the brown coat and red waistcoat of the Légion des Francs (Independent Legion) raised by Humbert for Hoche's expedition back in 1796. At that time Humbert dressed them in stocks of British red coats captured at Quiberon Bay, which were re-dyed a very dark, almost black shade of brown, re-cut in light infantry style, and embellished with light blue facings. Known alternatively as either the Légion Noire (from their coats) or Légion Rouge (from their waistcoats), they had originally received slouched hats 'à la Henri IV', and close-fitting 'hussar-style' pale blue pantaloons, which were probably captured Hungarian breeches. This 1798 recruit has simply been given a pair of plain white linen trousers.

The flag carried by this, the most short-lived of the Irish Brigades, appears to have been green with the traditional gold harp and motto *Erin go Bragh* ('Ireland Forever'), but with the crown replaced by a 'cap of liberty'. The same flag, or one very like it, was also picked up in the aftermath of Robert Emmet's abortive rising in Dublin five years later.

INDEX

References to illustrations are shown in **bold**.
Plates are shown with page and caption locators in brackets.